THE
CONSUMER'S
GUIDE TO

FEEDING
REPTILES

All About What's in Reptile Food, Why It's There and How to Choose the Best Food for Your Pet

LIZ PALIKA

HOWELL
BOOK
HOUSE
New York

Howell Book House

A Simon & Schuster/Macmillan Company
1633 Broadway
New York, NY 10019

Library of Congress Cataloging-in-Publication Data

Palika, Liz, 1954-
   The consumer's guide to feeding reptiles   all about what's in reptile food, why it's there, and how to choose the best food for your pet/Liz Palika.
        p.   cm.
Includes bibliographical references (p. 129) and index.

ISBN 0-87605-681-8

   1. Reptiles as pets--Feeding and feeds.   2. Reptiles as pets--
Nutrition.   3. Consumer education.   I. Title.
SF459.R4P34   1996
639.3'9--dc21   96-49678
                                                        CIP

Manufactured in the United States of America
10 9 8 7 6 5 4 3 2 1

CONTENTS

DIRECTORY OF CHARTS

INTRODUCTION

As a young teenager, I remember coming home with a very large black racer (snake). When I tried to show it to my mother, she promptly locked me out of the house until my father came home from work. I couldn't understand her horror. However, I didn't keep any reptiles as pets until I got married. In fact, when my new husband moved into my apartment, he brought several snakes with him.

Over the years our menagerie grew. We have owned king snakes, boas and pythons; anoles, iguanas and monitors; Argentine horned frogs and fire bellied toads; box turtles and sulcattas; even a caiman. Today we have over 50 reptiles, but the count changes daily since we are breeding Gulf Coast box turtles, leopard tortoises and Jackson Chameleons.

Many people ask me why I like reptiles. Perhaps I see in them a relationship to the dinosaurs. In fact, if you watch the movie *Jurassic Park*, look closely at the heads of the velociraptors. Then look closely at the head of a tiny anole. See the similarities? I realize that *Jurassic Park* is a movie with made-up dinosaurs, but it is the way I see them in my imagination.

Reptiles also continually surprise me. I love to watch a reptile of mine and see a personality emerge. My leopard tortoises all have individual personalities, as do the Russian tortoises. Even our two Argentine horned frogs differ from one another. I think people assume the animal has no personality because they do not watch it or give it enough of a chance.

Keeping reptiles for the last 20 years has also been a challenge. For many years it was very difficult to find reliable information about the care and feeding of many reptiles. It was also hard to make sure you were feeding your reptile properly. In the mid-1970s, my husband and I lost 10 newborn Jackson Chameleons because we couldn't find any fruit flies or pinhead crickets. I had saucers of mashed bananas everywhere, trying to attract fruit flies. But even in Southern California, there aren't many fruit flies in December.

So this book, which is the third in a series (following *The Consumer's Guide to Dog Food* and *The Consumer's Guide to Cat Food*), grew out of a desire to never again be faced with the death of a pet due to lack of information. I hope this information helps you, too, and your treasured pets.

Liz Palika

ONE

REPTILES AND REPTILE FOOD

Reptiles have long had a very tentative relationship with people.

Snakes especially have suffered at humanity's hands since the beginning of recorded history. Who hasn't heard the story of the serpent that ruined Adam and Eve's relationship? And how about Cleopatra using an asp (a venomous snake) to commit suicide?

Greek mythology portrayed Medusa, whose hair was a multitude of writhing snakes, as the most evil of creatures. However, the Greeks were one of the few ancient cultures that also saw good in the snake. Ironically, the snake's ability to shed its skin was what the Greeks so much admired. Greek literature shows us that the serpent's ability to shed its skin without dying was like shedding old age and starting all over again.

OUR HISTORY WITH FROGS

Moses inflicted snakes, frogs and locusts as plagues on Pharaoh. Locusts might be a problem, and some types of snakes certainly will be, but frogs? Other cultures have been and are afraid of frogs, too, though. Many South American native people believe that the Argentine horned frogs are aggressive, dangerous and evil. Called *escuerzos*, these frogs are associated with superstition, sorcery and black magic.

Although frogs are generally not feared in the same way as snakes, nor regarded historically as bad omens as snakes were, frogs have had their share of bad times. In the Dark Ages, a dried toad placed on the boils of a plague victim was supposed to be healing. It might have been healing to the person, but it certainly wasn't healing for the toad! In literature, many of the recipes that witches used to cast spells included frogs, toads, lizards and their respective body parts.

Ironically, frogs and toads were also believed to be good luck. If newlyweds saw a toad in the roadway on their way to their honeymoon, they would have a happy marriage. Gamblers believe that if you see a frog on your way to the game, you will have good luck. Farmers used to believe that it was bad luck to kill a frog; if you did, your cow would die.

OUR HISTORY WITH LIZARDS

The lizard has had a tough time, too. Ancient healers used a drink laced with boiled lizard tails that was supposed to cure the common cold, heal boils and lower fevers. In southeast Africa, it is still believed that the lizard is God's messenger and comes to tell certain people that there will be no life after death. The people of that region despise and kill lizards.

TURTLES & TORTOISES, BRIEFLY

Although they have often been eaten for food, as a general rule turtles and tortoises have had a better time throughout history. Many ancient societies viewed the turtle (or tortoise) as the animal that carried the world on its back. The turtle has also been regarded as the symbol of long life and wisdom by many people.

DOMESTICATING REPTILES

Although dogs have been domesticated for many thousands of years and cats have been living with people off and on for close to 6,000 years, only recently have reptiles been kept as pets in large numbers. Ancient history mentions some specific instances of reptile pet ownership, especially in ancient Greece and Egypt, but for the most part, reptiles have been kept successfully as pets only in the past century.

In this century, and most notably the past twenty years, people have become more aware that the supply of animals in the wild is finite. In the past, if a particular snake in someone's collection died (for whatever reasons) another was caught in the wild to replace it. In addition, because so little was known about proper care, very few of the reptiles in captivity many years ago reproduced successfully.

TAKING CARE OF WHAT WE'VE GOT

However, with many species extinct, endangered or threatened, and more natural reptile habitats being destroyed, more research is being done to satisfy the needs of the animals in captivity. When a reptile owner can properly care for a particular snake, frog, newt or lizard, then there is more chance that that animal will live a longer, healthier life and perhaps even reproduce.

Captive reptile breeding has grown tremendously in the past twenty years, again because research has shown that supplying the proper environment, conditions and nutrition for a particular animal can eliminate some of the stress of captivity and make it possible for the animals to reproduce. Captive breeding has made it possible for more people to own reptiles as pets by producing those animals in a safe, healthy environment.

Reptiles caught in the wild are always stressed to some extent by their capture and the change in their environment, some more than others. They may also be loaded with parasites or suffer from injuries or disease. However, when raised by a knowledgeable breeder, captive-bred reptiles are normally healthy, parasite-free and well adapted to their captive environment.

As we have seen, the relationship between humanity and reptiles has had its ups and downs, depending upon the times and the society involved. At times the reptile was worshipped, while in other times people became the reptile's worst danger.

Today, humanity is still many reptiles' greatest danger; but, overall, life for many species is looking up. More and more people each year own reptiles as pets and treasure them as companions. Veterinary care has also improved and knowledge of reptile needs is increasing so that owners can provide the proper environment for their pets. New products arrive in stores regularly—products that provide safe heat, humidity, light and so on, all of which help pet owners care for their pets. And our knowledge of nutrition is improving, too, so that reptile owners can feed their pets better.

REPTILE FOOD

For as long as reptiles have existed, they have hunted or foraged for themselves. Some snakes hunted mice, rats or other rodents, while others hunted lizards, frogs, small fish, or even other snakes. Some snakes even ate eggs. Lizards caught bugs or other lizards, or grazed on tree leaves, blossoms and fruit. Frogs ate insects, small mice or each other. Instinctively, each species followed certain guidelines as to what it should eat.

However, captivity changed that. Now a snake used to eating small fish may be offered a mouse. What is it supposed to do? If by chance it does eat the mouse, then what? Can a snake that is genetically programmed to eat fish suddenly change to mice and thrive? Or will there be a nutritional problem later? This is just one issue researchers are facing as reptile pet ownership increases and the demand—and need—for answers grows with it. Many of these researchers work for commercial reptile food manufacturers, trying to develop products that supply reptiles' needs. But are they succeeding?

ABOUT COMMERCIAL PET FOODS

The first known commercial pet foods were prepared in England from the carcasses of horses that died in harness on London streets. Butchers would sell the leftovers—entrails, brains and other scraps—packaged especially for pet food.

In 1926 in the United States, the Purina Company established the Pet Care Center for testing new animal foods. The first Purina dog food, Dog Chow Checkers, was introduced and received rave reviews from Admiral Richard Byrd, who used it to feed his sled dogs in Antarctica. Since Purina already had a reputation for producing good food for domestic animals, especially swine, dog owners were willing to give the new food a try.

After World War II the idea really caught on. Prepared pet foods were a convenience, just like drive-through restaurants and frozen dinners, and those conveniences were much sought after by American women after the war.

Most of the early pet foods were meat-based foods, usually beef or horsemeat. Meat scraps were readily available and inexpensive, and it was widely believed by pet owners that dogs and cats needed to eat meat. Although many grains and other nonmeat sources of nutrition were available to pet food manufacturers, often at a lower cost than meat, these ingredients were not often used since researchers of the time believed that dogs did not have the necessary digestive enzymes to break down the crude fiber or cellulose present in grains, beans, seeds and many vegetables.

Things changed again in 1956 when a research team working for the Purina Company developed a controllable cooking process called extrusion. Extrusion cooking allowed feed grains to be used in pet foods for the first time. Dr. Thomas Willard, a nutritional consultant, said, "Extrusion cooking adds a crunchy texture to the food for better palatability, and is the single most important development in the pet food industry since man first tossed a wild canine a bone over 20,000 years ago." (*AKC Gazette*, "What Are We Really Feeding Our Dogs?" July 1992.)

By the mid-1970s, prepackaged pet foods had become big business. Today they are a $1.75-billion industry. In many grocery stores, pet foods cover more aisle and shelf space than do baby foods.

COMMERCIAL REPTILE FOOD

Prepackaged reptile foods began appearing in specialty pet stores over a period of time. Some of the early foods were repackaged (relabeled) aquarium fish foods, and their nutritive quality was questionable. However, the late 1980s and early to mid-1990s saw a great increase in the number of prepackaged reptile foods. There were more foods available for different kinds of reptiles, and there were more forms of foods available. There were foods for carnivorous (meat-eating), herbivorous (plant-eating) and omnivorous (meat- and plant-eating) reptiles. Sources of live foods became more readily available for carnivores and insectivores as well.

SATISFYING REPTILES AND THEIR OWNERS

Why so many new foods? The reptile owner may buy the food for his or her pet, but the primary consumer is the reptile. A food that is not eagerly eaten will certainly not benefit the animal in any way. Of course, some reptiles will eat anything that is placed in front of them, but many more are discriminating about what they eat. Reptile owners are sure to notice when the lizard, snake or frog is not eating or is not eating the food with its normal relish.

Reptile owners want to be able to feed their animals food that is nutritionally balanced, affordable and relatively easy to feed. Reptile owners will go to incredible lengths to provide food for their pets, catching earthworms in the garden or chopping bowls of vegetables. However, if easier, healthy alternatives are available, many reptile owners will welcome them eagerly.

WHAT COMPANIES WANT

Most reptile food manufacturers have spent considerable time and money researching foods and developing new foods with four goals in mind:

1. To meet the needs of the reptile's owner
2. To make a food the reptile will readily eat
3. To make a food to meet the reptile's nutritional needs
4. To make a profit

RESEARCH AND MORE RESEARCH

The development of a reptile food is usually years in the making. Many factors come into play: What is the purpose or goal of this new food? Is it going to target a specific population, such as carnivorous reptiles? Is it good for omnivores, too? What are the proposed ingredients for this food? Are those ingredients readily available? What would the cost of these ingredients be? Who is the target consumer for this food?

When a recipe is proposed for a new food, the ingredients are then analyzed. What is the nutritional value of each ingredient and how do the ingredients work together? Will they meet or surpass the nutritional needs of the reptiles being fed?

Other factors in the recipe must also be researched. In what order should the ingredients be added? How long should the food be cooked and at what temperatures?

As test batches of the food are produced, they are sent back to the laboratory and further analyzed before final testing. If the food passes these tests, it is produced in limited quantities and fed to reptiles to test palatability (taste).

TESTING WHERE IT COUNTS: ON THE REPTILES

Ocean Nutrition, makers of the T-Rex brand reptile foods, maintains a feeding research center for reptiles. There, a population of iguanas is fed nothing but the T-Rex iguana food, while a small colony of snakes eats the new Snake Steak Sausage. Animals are monitored for growth, color and appearance, appetite and overall health. Food acceptance is also important.

Some reptile food manufacturers ask breeders, veterinarians, zoos or reptile owners to test new foods. The goal is to make sure the reptile will eagerly eat the food being offered and then will thrive on the food over a period of time.

PALATABILITY. At the Iams Animal Care Center, new cat foods are tested for palatability by giving the cat two bowls, each containing a different food. Technicians note which food was eaten first, which bowl was emptied first and, if any food was left over, which one. The test is repeated with the foods in different positions so the cat doesn't develop the habit of eating from one bowl first. Because a new food may attract (or, depending upon the cat, repel) simply because it is new or different, the tests are repeated for several days or even weeks to make sure the food has staying power.

Similar tests have been done with reptiles. A manufacturer of tortoise foods asked several tortoise breeders to conduct palatability tests with their food, with competitors' foods and with a diet of fresh foods including vegetables. By comparing results, the company was able to fine-tune its product so that more tortoises of different species would eagerly choose and eat the food.

DIGESTIBILITY. When a recipe for the new food has been tested for palatability and found acceptable, the food is then tested for digestibility. The reptiles' feces are analyzed so that the nutritional value of the food can be compared to the nutritional content of the feces. With these tests, technicians can determine how much nutritional value the reptile is actually getting from the food.

LONG-TERM FEEDING TESTS. If a new food makes it this far, it is next fed to various reptiles for a period of time, and detailed records are kept on the animals' health and well-being. Control studies are often done, comparing similar reptiles fed a known diet to the same species of reptiles fed the new diet. Researchers measure body weight, growth, blood profiles, skin condition, color and general health. These tests may run for six to nine months, or even as long as two years.

THE PRODUCT BEHIND THE PACKAGE

As the wise consumer, you must keep in mind that the reptile food companies are also in business to make a profit—and those profits are readily available. Pet foods are big business, and each company's goal is to get you to buy its food. This book will help you choose what's best for your reptile, no matter what the company claims.

TWO

NUTRITION AND GENERAL HEALTH

Throughout history, food in its various forms has been used as medicine. My grandmother seemed to think that chicken soup could cure just about any illness. Almost all human cultures have a number of foods—not just herbs, but everyday foods—that are recommended for certain circumstances. Recently, modern medicine has developed certain "magic bullets"—curatives such as aspirin, antibiotics and so on—that have replaced many of the ancient remedies by which humans survived for thousands of years.

THE PRICE OF PROCESSED FOODS

These magic bullets have indeed increased longevity and cured many diseases, but at what cost? People and their domestic animals are still suffering from malnutrition, and many researchers feel that our overly processed foods are to blame. We are, literally, cooking the nutrients out of our foods. Other researchers are recognizing more food allergies than were previously known, both in people and in our pets, and feel that this, too, is due to our reliance on processed foods. Obesity is also a major health hazard, for people and pets—even reptiles. The way to benefit from what modern medicine and commercial manufacturing processes offer us is to understand the basics of nutrition (the relationship between food and the health of the body). Proper nutrition means that all the body's essential nutrients—proteins, fats, carbohydrates, vitamins, minerals and, of course, water—are being supplied by the food that is being eaten, in a form that the reptile's body can use.

GOOD FOOD = GOOD HEALTH

Good nutrition is needed for a strong immune system, reproduction and normal growth. Food supplies the substances that act as regulators for the body's many processes, including organ development and functions and disease resistance. It also provides energy so that the body can function and live from day to day.

Because reptiles' diets are so varied depending on whether they are meat or plant eaters, feeding reptiles is a challenge. Specific foods or diets must be formulated for certain species to meet their individual nutritional needs.

Things that affect reptilian nutrition include

- the type of reptile
- its age
- its state of general health
- whether or not it is being used in a breeding program
- its activity level
- stress levels
- the food it normally eats

TYPE OF REPTILE. As was mentioned earlier, each type of reptile has certain nutritional needs: Some need meat; some need fish; some need fruits, pollen and greens; some need grasses. The variety is endless, and all these factors must be taken into account when formulating a diet for your reptile.

THE REPTILE'S AGE. Nutritional needs vary dramatically with the reptile's age. Active, rapidly growing reptiles often require more food or even significantly higher protein levels than do adult reptiles. Sometimes even the foods that are eaten may change. Hatchling box turtles will often refuse to eat anything except live foods, while adult box turtles will relish more fruits and vegetables.

STATE OF GENERAL HEALTH. Nutritional needs can vary dramatically depending upon the reptile's health. An animal stressed by injury or disease will need more support from a good food to provide for the increased needs of the immune system and for healing. A reptile with parasites will need medical attention to fight them off, and will need nutritional support to regain good health. Good nutrition can also work to prevent many health problems by keeping the immune system running properly.

THE IMPORTANCE OF LIGHT

Researchers specializing in human medicine discovered that many people suffer from a seasonal disorder that causes them to get depressed, moody and lethargic in the winter (Seasonal Affective Disorder, or SAD). It was found that these people are affected by the shorter daylight hours, less sun and increased cloud cover. When exposed to lights of a specific type, the effects of this disorder could be greatly reduced.

Light is even more important to reptiles. In the wild, sunlight provides heat, which stimulates the appetite and allows the reptile to digest its food. Natural photoperiods are also important. A light should never be left on for twenty-four hours; instead, a natural photoperiod of twelve on and twelve off is preferred. If you decide to breed your animals, you may have to adjust the photoperiod even more to mimic natural daylight hours.

The sun's natural UVB rays also allow the reptile to synthesize vitamin D3. This vitamin is necessary to metabolize calcium; without D3, calcium would simply pass through the body unused, causing innumerable health problems.

In captivity, reptiles still need these rays. If the reptile is exposed to several hours of unfiltered light per week, those needs will be satisfied. However, if the reptile is caged inside, you must provide the needed UVB rays through artificial light. Not all light bulbs produce the needed light.

Zoo Med has produced a fluorescent light called Repti Iguana Light UVB 310, which is designed specifically for iguanas. Zoo Med states that this light produces the complete ultraviolet spectrum present in sunlight in the tropics at noon. National Biological Corporation also produces a fluorescent light (Reptile D-Light) that duplicates natural sunlight with a full 8 percent UVB concentration. Because UVB rays are produced by fluorescent lights, which do not provide heat, many reptile enclosures will need two light sources: one fluorescent light to produce the needed UVB rays, plus an incandescent light for UVA rays and heat.

SOURCES OF REPTILE LIGHT

Company	Phone No.	Product
Chromolux	800-788-5781	Incandescent, heat lights
Durolite	Find at your local pet store	Incandescent, fluorescent and basking lights
MTS Electronics	610-588-6011	Fluorescent lights
National Biological	800-891-5218	Fluorescent lights
Reptile Lights	310-784-2770	Incandescent, fluorescent and heat lights
Zoo Med	Find at your local pet store	Fluorescent, heat/basking and incandescent lights

REPRODUCTION. Good nutrition is necessary for both the male and the female, both prior to and during breeding. The male that is not well nourished may not produce viable sperm and may even have a reduced desire to breed. If the female is not well nourished, she may not ovulate properly, may not release eggs or may not have the reserves herself to adequately nourish the eggs or the growing embryos. During gestation, the female will be robbing her own body of nutrients to satisfy the growing embryos' needs. It's important that her state of health prior to breeding is good and that her nutritional needs are met.

ACTIVITY LEVELS. Some reptiles are by nature less active than others. Some snakes perch themselves on a branch and wait for their prey to appear before them, as do many frogs. Other reptiles actively search for their prey. Some herbivores, like tortoises, often browse for hours, two or three times a day, looking for the best food. The reptiles that are more active need nutritional support from their food to maintain this activity level.

STRESS. Stress for a reptile can be caused by many things; it can be the change from being wild to being in captivity (including the stress of capture itself, shipping and several changes in location). In captivity, stress could be a change in its cage, a change in the location of its cage, a change in cage companions or a change in owners or caretakers. Stress can come from the environment, too, including high noise levels, improper lighting, incorrect humidity and more.

Although good nutrition can help some animals deal better with stress, reptiles are notorious for their sensitivity, and for some reptiles no amount of good food can overcome the stress. Humidity is a good example. Although mammals can tolerate extremes in humidity, many reptiles cannot. Most amphibians and many lizards require very specific levels of humidity; if those needs are not met, the animal will die, no matter their diet.

FOOD. The food your reptile is eating can cause stress, too, especially if it is of poor quality, made of ingredients that are not easily digestible or is simply not the right food for your reptile. Too much or too little food can be a problem, too, for obvious reasons.

FOOD AND THE BODY

As you can see, there is no single thing that can ensure good health. For most reptiles, good health requires proper food, correct lighting, adequate temperatures, proper humidity and a secure cage of the right size and type. An environment relatively free of physical dangers, excess chemicals and insecticides will also aid in the maintenance of good health. And, of course, good nutrition is an important part of the puzzle.

WHAT IF YOUR REPTILE WON'T EAT?

Many pet owners have been traumatized by their reptile's unwillingness to eat and, unfortunately, there is no easy answer to the problem. Reptiles will not eat, or will stop eating, for a number of different reasons. The stress of capture, shipment and captivity may cause an animal to reject food. A simple lack of familiar food could be the problem. Disease and/or parasites could cause anorexia. Improper husbandry practices, especially regarding temperature and humidity, are common problems. Some reptiles show more interest after being misted with water, or after soaking in warm (slightly cooler than lukewarm) water or after basking in the sun.

THE IMPORTANCE OF HEAT

Reptiles rely on external sources for heat. This heat is necessary to stimulate appetite, to digest food and to maintain a healthy immune system. Without proper heat, the body's processes will slow and the reptile will be unable to fight off disease. In the rare cases when the reptile doesn't succumb to disease, it will starve to death.

Most captive reptiles are dependent upon the ambient temperature—the temperature of their enclosure—to stimulate an interest in eating. With a few exceptions, reptiles will not eat if the temperature is below 65 degrees or above 90 degrees.

If a reptile is too cool, it may hibernate (depending upon the species) or it will die. Box turtles, for example, will hibernate when the weather cools down in the fall or winter. Green iguanas, however, come from a more tropical climate and will not hibernate; if they get too cold for too long, they will die.

Digestion is also affected by temperature. Green iguanas and herbivorous tortoises, for example, require high temperatures to adequately digest their food. A basking area heated to 90 degrees will be used frequently as the animal digests its meal. Many other reptiles are the same; some snakes will not digest their prey if too cool and the food can actually become toxic in the digestive system.

Temperature needs vary among species. The optimum temperature—the best temperature for eating, digestion and good health—for most reptiles is 88 degrees Fahrenheit. Geckos, bearded dragons, swifts and many other lizards will thrive at 80 to 88 degrees. Most boa constrictors and pythons do well at 84 to 88 degrees.

However, there are exceptions. King snakes, milk snakes and garter snakes like to be slightly cooler; the best temperature for them would be between 75 and 80 degrees. Argentine horned frogs do well at 80 degrees Fahrenheit with a nighttime drop to 75 degrees. Jackson chameleons do well at 75 to 80 degrees during the day with a nighttime drop to 60 degrees.

There are a variety of ways to provide this heat. An incandescent light bulb mounted above the screen on top of an enclosure (or cage) works well. The wattage of the bulb would depend upon the needs of the reptile and the size of the cage. A small thermometer inside the cage can gauge the temperature.

Reptile supply companies also offer a number of different alternatives for providing heat. There are heat rocks—artificial rocks with heating elements inside—that come preset at different temperatures. Heat rocks are particularly good for reptiles that like to bask in the sun, such as some lizards and snakes. There are also heating pads that attach to the bottom of a glass terrarium; these, too, come preset or with temperature controls. There are also ceramic heaters that screw in to a light bulb socket, as well as a variety of different types of light bulbs.

No matter which of the heating options you use, it is important to provide a warm section of the enclosure and a cooler area that the reptile can move to should it get too warm. Most reptiles will move back and forth, regulating their temperature according to their needs.

SOURCES OF HEATING DEVICES

Company	Phone No.	Product
Clark	405-722-5017	Thermostats
Durolite	Find at your local pet store	Basking, heat lights
Fluker Labs	504-343-7035	Heat rocks, under-cage heaters
Hagen	Find at your local pet store	Under-cage heaters
Helix Controls	619-566-8335	Thermostats, temperature controls, heating systems
JS Technologies	818-353-1577	Thermostats
Ocean Nutrition	619-336-4728	Thermometers
Ram Network	818-345-0484	Ceramic bulb heaters
Zoo Med	Find at your local pet store	Heat rocks, temperature controls

Other reptiles seem to fast naturally. Most snakes will not eat just prior to shedding. Other female snakes (and some lizards and tortoises) will fast just before laying eggs or giving birth. Some reptiles will fast just prior to hibernation or estivation. A few species are known for being poor eaters. Ball pythons are notoriously poor eaters, and will often fast for months at a time.

When a reptile refuses to eat and all possible techniques have been tried to encourage the animal to eat (see Chapter 12 for advice), then veterinary intervention is necessary. Don't wait until the animal is weak and starved, however; it may never recover.

ELIMINATION PROBLEMS

CONSTIPATION. Because of their differences, elimination varies in reptiles, which can make it difficult to judge whether or not an animal is constipated or blocked. Ultimately, it is up to you to know the normal habits of each particular animal and keep track of eliminations.

Snakes that eat mice or rats may defecate after each feeding, or may defecate after every third or fourth feeding, depending upon the size of the snake and the size of the prey animals. If the snake is switched over to a mouse-substitute food, there might be a change in elimination habits because with the substitute foods there are no bones or fur to digest or pass. At the other extreme, tortoises that graze daily are consuming vast amounts of fiber and may defecate copious amounts of feces daily.

When the owner is knowledgeable of the animal's normal habits, a change is easy to spot and prompt attention can sometimes prevent disaster. Sometimes a warm bath can help stimulate the intestinal tract. If that isn't successful, contact your veterinarian as soon as possible.

DIARRHEA. Change in diet can sometimes cause diarrhea. Too much fruit can cause loose stools in many herbivores, especially if the animal doesn't normally consume much fruit. Unfortunately, diarrhea in reptiles is often a sign that the animal is suffering from internal parasites of some kind, or is hosting some protozoan, bacterial or other disease-causing organisms. Again, veterinary assistance should be sought or the animal may become dehydrated.

GASTROINTESTINAL DISORDERS. Gastrointestinal disorders can be caused by a variety of problems, including parasites, infections, metabolic imbalances, tumors or injuries. Most wild-caught reptiles have an assortment of parasites and must be checked carefully by a veterinarian who specializes in reptiles. It is also amazing what some reptiles will eat, especially if the animal is allowed some freedom, in either the house or the backyard. Iguanas and tortoises have been known to eat many strange things, including pieces of silk plants, coins and strings, even rocks.

Some gastrointestinal disorders are caused by the food the reptile eats. A reptile that eats a diseased or malnourished mouse or a snail that was exposed to snail bait could very well suffer the effects.

METABOLIC BONE DISEASE. Metabolic bone disease (MBD), also called nutritional secondary hyperparathyroidism, is the most commonly diagnosed condition in green iguanas. MBD shows itself by several different clinical signs, including thin, weak bones; swollen, misshapen lower jaws; and limb, back and tail fractures. Untreated animals will suffer broken bones, will become progressively weaker and will eventually die.

Veterinarians can confirm a diagnosis by checking the blood-calcium levels. X-rays can also be helpful. A new treatment used with good results is the administration of a synthetic hormone, calcitonin-salmon, a polypeptide hormone secreted by the thyroid gland in mammals. It works in different ways, but its primary goal is to help rebuild bone quickly.

MBD can be prevented through proper nutrition, making sure that the animal eats a well-balanced diet that has a calcium-phosphorus ratio of 2:1. The iguana also needs full-spectrum light (see page 11) or a few hours weekly of direct, unfiltered light.

OBESITY. Obesity is one of the newest problems in reptiles. Rarely are animals in the wild obese. However, reptiles that find food placed in front of them on a regular basis will, naturally, eat the food, and in the process will use no calories finding or hunting the food. Overweight reptiles are more prone to a variety of health problems, depending upon the species. Because this is a relatively new problem to reptiles, the full extents of the dangers are only now becoming known.

POISONS. Because many reptiles normally eat by browsing or hunting for their food, they can also fall victim to a variety of poisons. If your iguana has the run of your house, or of one room, make sure that all your houseplants are nontoxic. Tortoises are especially vulnerable because they often have the run of their owner's backyard and may unwittingly sample poisonous plants, such as an oleander leaf.

Other poisons are commonly found around our homes. Don't feed your box turtles snails from your yard if you or any of your neighbors put out snail bait. Don't pick rose blossoms for your iguana or tortoise if you routinely spray with fungicides or insecticides. Do you spray your house for ants or fleas? Those sprays could kill your reptile, too, if you aren't careful.

THYROID. Hyperthyroidism is the overproduction of hormones by the thyroid gland. Symptoms might include nervousness, fatigue, weight loss and rapid pulse. Hypothyroidism is the underproduction of hormones and results in decreased appetite, dull, dry skin, clumsiness, lack of vigor, and in breeding males, lowered sperm count.

Although both types of thyroid disease can be inherited, nutrition can also be a factor. Many foods contain soybeans and soybean meal, both of which are incomplete protein sources, lacking several essential amino acids. If this loss isn't made up for with other ingredients, this amino acid loss could lead to a lack of tyrosine, the amino acid that stimulates the thyroid gland to produce more hormones. Although studies investigating this relationship are continuing, reptiles with thyroid disease or a genetic predisposition to it should not be fed commercial foods high in soy.

EATING RIGHT FOR A LIFETIME

Although many things contribute to how long a reptile will live, including its species, heredity, environment and general health, good nutrition has been linked by several studies to longevity. A diet that supplies the reptile's nutritional needs is imperative to good health, which goes hand in hand with long life.

THREE

THE BASIC BUILDING BLOCKS
OF FOOD

There are eight basic building blocks of nutrition present in the food your reptile eats. They are

- water
- enzymes
- protein
- carbohydrates
- fats
- fiber
- vitamins
- minerals

These nutrients contain chemical substances that affect the body. They might provide the body with energy, or they might assist in the regulation of body processes, or they might provide for the growth and repair of tissues.

Each of these nutrient building blocks has its own purpose, its own function, but it does not work alone. All these nutrients are required, in varying amounts, for a well-balanced diet. The amounts needed depend upon the reptile and factors like age, general health, activity level and environment (discussed in Chapter 2).

In this chapter we will discuss six of the eight basic building blocks: water, enzymes, protein, carbohydrates, fats and fiber. In Chapter 4 we will continue with vitamins and minerals.

WATER: THE MAGIC LIQUID

A simple substance, water is one of the most abundant and important resources of our planet and one that is taken for granted more than anything else. However, without water, life as we know it would cease to exist.

The body of most reptiles is approximately two thirds water. Blood is slightly over 80 percent water, muscles are over 70 percent water and the brain is almost 75 percent water. Even bones are 20 percent water.

Water is required for the normal functioning of every cell in the body. Respiration, digestion, metabolism and elimination all require water. Water is needed to dissolve and transport nutrients. Water keeps all things in balance; only oxygen is more necessary to preserve life.

A certain amount of water is lost each day through respiration and elimination and must be replaced. Some desert reptiles, especially some lizards, have a tough skin that is impervious to the elements and does not lose water. The amount of water needed by each reptile can vary depending upon the species involved, the reptile's size, its activity level and the climate, especially the temperature and humidity.

The type of reptile also will determine its method of elimination and how much water is lost during elimination. For example, many tortoises excrete a fairly bulky, somewhat drier stool and chalky urine. In comparison, water turtles pass a more fluid urine and softer, less bulky stools.

Water needs can also vary depending upon the natural climate of the reptile. Many desert reptiles have been genetically programmed to conserve water and may go for months or even years without actually drinking. Instead water might be obtained from the food that is consumed, or the animal might estivate, becoming dormant for the summer, through a heat spell or during a drought. Many desert reptiles can even "recycle" water from urinary wastes.

Other reptiles require more water, both in the air as humidity and to drink. Jackson Chameleons, a popular and attractive chameleon now being bred in captivity quite successfully, requires a water drip system in its enclosure so that it can take in drops of water as needed. Before this was known, many Jackson Chameleons died with full water bowls in their cages. These chameleons do not know how to drink out of a bowl; instead, they are genetically programmed to look for water falling from leaves.

WATER, WATER, WATER!

All reptiles need water to some extent, but how much and in what form varies according to the individual species. Turtles that live in water, for example, such as the spiney softshell turtle or the red-eared slider, of course need more water than does the California desert tortoise, which obtains much of its water needs from the plants it eats. But there is more to water than simply how much water is needed; the reptile keeper—you—must also supply water in a way that the reptile can use.

Some reptiles will readily use a water bowl, recognizing it as a source of water. Most snakes will drink from a bowl of water and will also soak in the water if the bowl is big enough. Many lizards, frogs and toads will use a bowl as long as there is easy access both into and out of it. Many reptiles will drown if the bowl is too deep or is slick or slippery, so the bowl must be shallow or there must be traction of some kind, like rocks to climb on. If the bowl is accessible, turtles and tortoises will also learn to use a bowl, although turtles and tortoises have also been known to drown in bowls that were too deep or too slippery. Because of this, and because of the mobility problems caused by an inflexible shell, tortoises can drink much easier out of a low bowl or saucer, such as those placed under houseplants.

Some reptiles need a bowl or terrarium big enough to allow soaking or even swimming constantly, like water turtles, fire bellied toads, frogs, some newts and axolotyls. You can use an aquarium filtration system to keep the water clean and circulating. Other reptiles, such as some snakes, iguanas and box turtles, need soaking on a regular basis but don't necessarily need to have a big bowl constantly.

One drawback to leaving a bowl of water in the enclosure all the time is that many reptiles will eliminate in their water—turtles and iguanas are known to do this. Although it can make housekeeping easier, the water must be changed daily to prevent a buildup of bacteria and the spread of disease.

Water should not be left in the enclosures of desert reptiles, as it will cause too much humidity. This could lead to a number of health problems, including respiratory disease and death. Instead, water should be offered two or three times a week, and removed after an hour or so.

Tropical reptiles generally need more humidity than do other reptiles, and that humidity can be supplied by water in the enclosure or by misting or spraying the enclosure. Many tropical reptiles drink their water by lapping droplets off leaves. Anoles, chameleons and iguanas especially will take much of their water this way. Anoles have been known to die of dehydration with a water bowl in their enclosure; these tiny lizards simply don't know how to drink from a bowl—they need water droplets from misting.

A tropical enclosure can also be set up with a drip system to supply this needed water. A small plastic container on top of the enclosure can be fitted with an air tube (hose) and a regulator/shut-off valve from an aquarium supply store that will allow a slow drip of water to fall onto some plants in the enclosure. A bowl or tray under the enclosure can catch the excess water. The reptiles can then lap water droplets as they need to.

ENZYMES: THE ESSENTIAL BUILDING BLOCKS

Enzymes have numerous essential functions in the reptile's body; so many, in fact, that the reptile cannot live without them. Enzymes are made up of two parts: One part is the protein molecule and the other is called the coenzyme. This coenzyme may be a vitamin or a chemical derivative of a vitamin. Enzymes work by initiating a chemical reaction so that other substances can do their job.

The digesting and metabolizing of food require a complex system of enzymes to make sure that thousands of different chemical reactions happen as they should. In the digestive processes, an enzyme is capable of breaking down one specific substance. For example, an enzyme designed to break down carbohydrates does not metabolize fats and the enzyme that breaks down milk products does not break down carbohy-drates. By "breaking down" the food, the nutrients in the food then become available for use by the body.

Because enzymes are made up of proteins and other substances, usu-ally a vitamin, the number of enzymes available for use by the reptile can vary and can depend upon the reptile's diet.

PROTEIN: THE FOUNDATION FOOD

Next to water, protein is the most plentiful element in an animal's body, representing approximately 50 percent of each cell. Proteins are incredibly diverse, and serve as building blocks of claws, skin, muscle, tendons, cartilage and other connective tissues. Protein is one of the most important elements of food for growth, development and repair of body tissues, sexual development and metabolism. Proteins are also vital parts of the bloodstream, the immune system, the digestive system, hormone production and much, much more.

Different species of reptiles need varying amounts of protein. Snakes that eat whole mice are consuming much more protein than green iguanas that can live an entire life eating only green vegetable matter and an occasional insect. The one-pound box turtle that eats worms, insects and carrion is consuming much more protein than the twenty-pound tortoise grazing on grass. Each of these species is, again, genetically programmed to eat its unique diet.

AMINO ACIDS. During digestion, amino acids are formed when large protein molecules are broken down by chemical action into smaller molecules. Amino acids are interesting molecules; they are both the end process of protein digestion and also the molecules from which proteins can be constructed.

Amino acids are vital to the transmission of nerve impulses, and as a result are needed for muscular contractions and for the electrical impulses in the brain and spinal cord. Amino acids are involved in the formation of DNA and in the functioning of the immune system. The body's chemistry is so interwoven and so dependent upon other substances and chemicals that an imbalance of even one amino acid can throw the whole system out of kilter.

COMPLETE AND INCOMPLETE PROTEINS. Protein sources that contain all the amino acids, such as lean meat and whole eggs, are called complete protein sources. Sources of protein that do not contain all the amino acids, such as soybean, wheat or corn, are called incomplete proteins.

Besides being a major building block in your reptile's body, protein can also be used as a source of energy. When carbohydrates are not available for use by the body in times of need, protein can be metabolized in their place. In addition, excess protein that is not needed for body functioning or repair can be converted into fat by the liver and stored for future use.

GETTING THE AMOUNT RIGHT. As was just mentioned, too much protein can be detrimental to your reptile's health. Too much protein can have potentially serious results, including possible kidney failure. Therefore, excess protein is not advised—more is *not* better in this situation.

Protein deficiencies may result in growth abnormalities, especially skeletal deformities. The skin may also be affected, depending upon the extent of the deficiency. Protein deficiency may also show up as a lack of energy and stamina, mental dullness and even depression. With protein deficiency, there will also be a noted weakness of the immune system and the reptile will be open to infection and disease.

SOURCES OF PROTEIN. The reptile that consumes live foods such as insects, mice or rats will obtain all the necessary protein from those foods.

Commercial prepackaged reptile foods supply protein from a number of different sources; some, as discussed above, are complete proteins, containing all the essential amino acids, while others are not. Along the same lines, some of the protein sources are more digestible (more usable) by the reptile than others. For these and other reasons (including cost to the manufacturer and availability) most reptile foods have more than one source of protein.

Beef, chicken, turkey and lamb meat are the most common meat sources of protein. Frequently, reptile foods also use fish as a protein source. Meat by-products—meat and bone meal, liver, organ meats and other meat products—are also protein sources, as are eggs.

Many different vegetable proteins are also commonly used, including wheat in various forms (whole wheat, wheat germ, wheat flour), corn, rice, soy, barley and other grains. Some reptile foods will include alfalfa meal, carrots, peas, beans or potatoes.

CARBOHYDRATES: THE ENERGY BUILDING BLOCK

Carbohydrates are the major element in most plants, accounting for 60 to 75 percent of the dry-matter weight of plants. Like proteins, when eaten, carbohydrates have more than one use in the reptile's body:

- Carbohydrates supply energy for bodily functions and are needed to assist in the digestion of other foods.
- Carbohydrates help regulate protein and are one of the most important sources of energy for muscular exertion.

Most carbohydrates present in foods are sugars, starches and cellulose.

SUGARS AND STARCHES. Sugars and starches are easily digested and are converted to a simple sugar, such as glucose. This is used by the body as fuel for the muscles, as well as for the brain and the nervous system. Excess glucose (sugar from plant material) is converted to glycogen and is stored in the liver and muscles for future use.

CELLULOSE. This material is not easily digested by carnivores and serves as fiber for water regulation in the intestinal tract, aiding in the formation and elimination of feces. However, herbivores, with a slower digestive metabolism, easily digest and metabolize cellulose.

SOURCES OF CARBOHYDRATES. Vegetables and grains that supply proteins to the reptile can also be a good source of carbohydrates. Corn, rice, oats, potatoes and wheat are easily digested after processing, even by many carnivores, and are good sources of carbohydrates.

FATS: A NECESSARY BUILDING BLOCK

Dietary fats, called lipids, are a group of compounds that are not soluble in water and have a number of different functions in the reptile's body. Some lipids are a part of cell structures; others are a part of the blood plasma. Lipids serve as carriers for the fat-soluble vitamins—A, D, E and K.

Fats are also involved in many different chemical processes in the body. Fatty layers under the skin serve as insulation against heat loss. An important component of lipids are the fatty acids. The alpha-linolenate acids are three fatty acids—oleic, linoleic and linolenic—that cannot be manufactured by the animal's body and must be supplied by food. They are necessary for normal growth, healthy blood, arteries and nerves, and normal kidney function; and they keep the skin healthy and supple.

Fats are also a source of energy. Fats furnish more than twice the number of calories (or energy) per gram as do carbohydrates or protein.

As with many other dietary needs, different reptiles have different requirements for fat. Most herbivores require very little fat in their diet, and any addition of fat can have severe results. Insectivores and omnivores can digest slightly more fat than herbivores, but not much. Insects contain very little fat, so reptiles consuming insects as a primary food would not be expected to digest much fat. However, reptiles that eat carrion and reptiles that eat mice, rats or other mammals are bio-logically equipped to digest fat.

Too much fat can lead to obesity and its associated problems. Some snakes fed a diet of fat laboratory mice have had severe problems resulting from too much fat. Argentine horned frogs are often called Pac Man Frogs because they have such big mouths and because they love to eat. Obesity is a big problem with these frogs in captivity. These frogs will literally eat themselves to death if their owners cooperate.

A fat deficiency in a young animal will initially show up as slow growth. A rare fatty-acid deficiency may show up as liver disease, pan-creatitis or chronic digestive disorders.

SOURCES OF FATS. Reptiles that eat live prey will, again, get adequate amounts of fat from their prey. Commercial reptile foods usually have fat of some kind, most often animal fat, as one of their ingredients, with the amount of fat added calculated upon the needs of the animal for which the food was formulated. It is rarely a good idea to add any additional fat to the diet of any reptile.

FIBER: THE "ACTION" BUILDING BLOCK

Fiber is the part of food that is not digested by the reptile's body, such as hair and, in some species, cellulose. Just because it is not digested does not mean that it is worthless or wasted food, though. Fiber is nec-essary for good intestinal health by absorbing water and aiding in the formation and movement of feces.

BALANCING NUTRIENTS

All these nutrients work together, as do the other building blocks cov-ered in the next chapter. Each reptile species has its own dietary needs for protein, fat, carbohydrates and fiber, as well as the other nutrient building blocks, and we will discuss these in more detail in upcoming chapters.

CHART 1
COMMERCIAL DRY REPTILE FOOD
COMPARISONS

Supplement Name	Nutritional Information		Ingredients
Iguana Foods			
Kaytee Adult Iguana	Protein	12.5%	1. ground corn
Fortified Daily Diet	Fat	3%	2. oats
	Fiber	12%	3. alfalfa meal
	Moisture	12%	4. wheat
			5. wheat middlings

(Other ingredients of note: soybean meal, dried beet pulp, cane molasses, alfalfa leaves, dried sunflower petals, dried rose petals, added vitamins)

Nutri Grow Iguana	Protein	25%	1. soybean meal
Diet Growth Formula	Fat	2%	2. ground corn
	Fiber	14%	3. alfalfa meal
	Moisture	12%	4. corn gluten meal
			5. yeast culture

(Other ingredients of note: wheat meal and bran, oat bran, oyster shell, bone meal, added vitamins)

Nutri Grow Iguana Diet	Protein	18%	1. alfalfa meal
Maintenance Formula	Fat	2.5%	2. corn
	Fiber	16%	3. soybean meal
	Moisture	12%	4. germ meal
			5. wheat bran

(Other ingredients of note: dried yeast, oyster shell, bone meal, added vitamins)

CHART 1, CONTINUED

Supplement Name	Nutritional Information		Ingredients
Ocean Nutrition T-Rex Iguana Dry Adult Fruit & Flower Formula	Protein Fat Fiber Moisture	14% 3% 7% 10%	1. ground corn 2. ground wheat 3. oat groats 4. isolated protein 5. soyhulls

(Other ingredients of note: ground hibiscus flowers, added flavors, added vitamins)

Ocean Nutrition T-Rex Iguana Dry Adult Vegi Formula	Protein Fat Fiber Moisture	14% 3% 7% 10%	1. ground corn 2. ground wheat 3. oat groats 4. isolated protein 5. soy hulls

(Other ingredients of note: added flavors, added vitamins)

Ocean Nutrition T-Rex Iguana Juvenile Fruit & Flower Formula	Protein Fat Fiber Moisture	19% 5% 6% 10%	1. ground corn 2. ground wheat 3. oat groats 4. isolated proteins 5. soy hulls

(Other ingredients of note: ground hibiscus flowers, added flavors, added vitamins)

Pretty Pets Adult Iguana Food	Protein Fat Fiber Moisture	12% 3% 7% 10%	1. corn 2. wheat 3. oats 4. soy hulls 5. dicalcium phosphate

(Other ingredients of note: vegetable oils, added flavors, added vitamins)

Supplement Name	Nutritional Information		Ingredients
Zoo Med All Natural Iguana Food Adult Formula	Protein	12%	1. dried alfalfa
	Fat	4%	2. wheat bran
	Fiber	20%	3. soybean meal
	Moisture	15%	4. collard greens
			5. mustard greens

(Other ingredients of note: kale, spirulina, bee pollen, added vitamins)

Zoo Med All Natural Iguana Food Juvenile Formula	Protein	24%	1. dried alfalfa
	Fat	6%	2. wheat bran
	Fiber	12%	3. soybean meal
	Moisture	15%	4. collard greens
			5. mustard greens

(Other ingredients of note: kale, spirulina, bee pollen, beta carotene and other added vitamins)

Turtle and Tortoise Foods

Kaytee Land Turtle and Tortoise Fortified Daily Diet	Protein	14%	1. corn
	Fat	4%	2. oats
	Fiber	10%	3. wheat
	Moisture	12%	4. alfalfa meal
			5. wheat middlings

(Other ingredients of note: fishmeal, brewer's dried yeast, raspberries, strawberries, added vitamins)

Nutrafin Turtle Pellets	Protein	34%	1. fish meal
	Fat	4%	2. soy flour
	Fiber	2.5%	3. oat flour
	Moisture	10%	4. wheat flour
			5. shrimp

(Other ingredients of note: kelp, fish liver, yeast)

CHART 1, CONTINUED

Supplement Name	Nutritional Information		Ingredients
Ocean Nutrition T-Rex Box Turtle Dry Formula	Protein	23.2%	1. oats
	Fat	5.1%	2. corn
	Fiber	8.2%	3. ground corn
	Moisture	10%	4. corn meal
			5. soy protein

(Other ingredients of note: lamb meal, apple, peaches, added vitamins)

Ocean Nutrition T-Rex Tortoise Dry Formula	Protein	13%	1. corn
	Fat	3%	2. wheat middlings
	Fiber	10%	3. oats
	Moisture	12%	4. soy
			5. alfalfa meal

(Other ingredients of note: soy protein, cane molasses, added vitamins)

Tetra Terrafauna Reed's Iguana and Tortoise Food	Protein	20%	1. wheat middlings
	Fat	4%	2. soybean meal
	Fiber	15%	3. alfalfa meal
	Moisture	not listed	4. cane molasses
			5. salt

(Other ingredients of note: soybean oil, added vitamins)

Wardley Turtle Delight	Protein	50%	1. dried whole shrimp
	Fat	1.5%	
	Fiber	4%	
	Moisture	12%	

Zoo Med Zoo Menu Aquatic Turtle Food	Protein	30%	1. wheat flour
	Fat	5%	2. soybean meal
	Fiber	10%	3. fish meal
	Moisture	12%	4. soy oil
			5. ascorbic acid

(Other ingredients of note: added vitamins)

Supplement Name	Nutritional Information		Ingredients
Zoo Med Zoo Menu Box Turtle/Tortoise Food	Protein	18.4%	1. corn
	Fat	5.2%	2. soybean meal
	Fiber	8%	3. wheat
	Moisture	10%	4. alfalfa meal
			5. oats

(Other ingredients of note: molasses, limestone, soy oil, added vitamins)

Other Dry Reptile Foods

Nutri Grow Premium Diet Carnisaur	Protein	56%	1. poultry meal
	Fat	7%	2. oyster shell
	Fiber	5%	3. bone meal
	Moisture	12%	4. dried whole egg
			5. dried yeast

(Other ingredients of note: bee pollen, soybean meal, alfalfa meal, corn, wheat and oat bran, added vitamins)

Nutri Grow Premium Diet Herbisaur	Protein	23%	1. soybean meal
	Fat	3%	2. alfalfa meal
	Fiber	20%	3. ground corn
	Moisture	12%	4. corn gluten meal
			5. wheat germ meal

Nutri Grow Premium Diet Omnisaur	Protein	46%	1. poultry meal
	Fat	6%	2. soybean meal
	Fiber	10%	3. alfalfa meal
	Moisture	12%	4. wheat germ
			5. oyster shell

(Other ingredients of note: wheat and oat bran, yeast, egg, bone meal, added vitamins)

CHART 1, CONTINUED

Supplement Name	Nutritional Information		Ingredients
Tetra ReptoMin Floating Food Sticks	Protein	38%	1. fish meal
	Fat	5%	2. wheat starch
	Fiber	2%	3. torula dried yeast
	Moisture	8%	4. shrimp meal
			5. corn meal

(Other ingredients of note: dried potato products, ground brown rice, dried whey, algae meal, added vitamins)

CHART 2
COMMERCIAL REPTILE FOOD COMPARISONS, OTHER THAN DRY FOODS

Supplement Name	Nutritional Information		Ingredients
Ocean Nutrition Mice on Ice (frozen)	Protein	not given	1. whole mice
	Fat	not given	
	Fiber	not given	
	Moisture	not given	
Ocean Nutrition T-Rex Garter Grub (frozen)	Protein	18%	1. fish
	Fat	11.5%	2. meat
	Fiber	.5%	3. meat derivatives
	Moisture	67%	
Ocean Nutrition T-Rex Gecko Grub (frozen)	Protein	18%	1. meat
	Fat	10%	2. meat derivatives
	Fiber	.5%	
	Moisture	66.5%	
Ocean Nutrition T-Rex Monitor Munch (frozen)	Protein	21%	1. meat
	Fat	6.5%	2. meat derivatives
	Fiber	.5%	
	Moisture	67%	

Supplement Name	Nutritional Information		Ingredients
Ocean Nutrition T-Rex Snake Steak Sausage (frozen)	Protein Fat Fiber Moisture	16% 13% .4% 66%	1. meat 2. meat derivatives
San Francisco Bay Brand Iguana Veggie Burger (frozen)	Protein Fat Fiber Moisture	8.8% 2.5% 6.4% 63%	1. alfalfa meal 2. soy meal 3. wheat bran 4. apple fiber 5. rice gluten

(Other ingredients of note: tofu, oatmeal, carrots, brown rice, peas, bananas, molasses, figs, green beans, turnip greens, strawberries, mustard greens and more)

Supplement Name	Nutritional Information		Ingredients
Zoo Med Zoo Menu Box Turtle Food (canned)	Protein Fat Fiber Moisture	3% .5% 1% 78%	1. apple 2. corn meal 3. whole corn 4. dried carrot 5. dextrose

(Other ingredients of note: soybean meal, bone meal, brewer's yeast, kelp, added flavorings, added vitamins)

Supplement Name	Nutritional Information		Ingredients
Zoo Med Zoo Menu Iguana Food, Juvenile (canned)	Protein Fat Fiber Moisture	2.4% .5% 1% 78%	1. corn meal 2. dried apple 3. dried carrot 4. dextrose 5. soybean meal

(Other ingredients of note: brewer's yeast, kelp, added flavors, added vitamins)

CHART 2, CONTINUED

Supplement Name	Nutritional Information		Ingredients
Zoo Med Zoo Menu Iguana Food, Adult (canned)	Protein	1.2%	1. corn meal
	Fat	.5%	2. dried apple
	Fiber	1%	3. dried carrot
	Moisture	78%	4. dextrose
			5. bone meal

(Other ingredients of note: brewer's yeast, kelp, flavorings, added vitamins)

Zoo Med Zoo Menu Land Tortoise Food (canned)	Protein	3%	1. apple
	Fat	.5%	2. corn meal
	Fiber	1%	3. whole peas
	Moisture	78%	4. opuntia cactus
			5. dried carrot

(Other ingredients of note: dextrose, soybean meal, bone meal, brewer's yeast, kelp, added flavoring, added vitamins)

Zoo Med Repti-Cricket	Protein	71.7%	1. crickets
	Fat	3.9%	2. natural flavorings
	Fiber	8.9%	3. vitamin mix
	Moisture	5%	4. ascorbic acid
			5. folic acid

Zoo Med Zoo Menu Tegu Monitor Food (canned)	Protein	9%	1. soybean meal
	Fat	.5%	2. chicken
	Fiber	1%	3. corn meal
	Moisture	78%	4. wheat mill run
			5. kelp meal

(Other ingredients of note: bone meal, garlic powder, added vitamins)

FOUR

THE OTHER BUILDING BLOCKS

The discovery of vitamins in 1910 was one of the most exciting achievements in the field of nutrition. Prior to their discovery, researchers knew that some substances were needed for good health, but those substances were unknown. Although nutritionists and researchers have learned much about vitamins since their discovery, experts readily admit that there is still much that is unknown, including the amounts of many vitamins needed for good health.

For example, in 1970 Linus Pauling created an uproar in the nutritional and medical fields when his experiments showed that massive doses of vitamin C could prevent or cure many diseases in people. Research is still continuing, both for people and for our animals, and that research is constantly producing therapeutic applications for vitamins.

WHAT ARE VITAMINS AND WHAT DO THEY DO?

Vitamins are organic substances found only in plants and animals. With a few exceptions, the reptile's body cannot synthesize vitamins; therefore, vitamins must be supplied in food or in supplements.

In your reptile's body, vitamins function together and with enzymes and have a variety of different functions, including

- digestion
- metabolism
- growth
- reproduction
- cellular reproduction
- oxidation

Vitamins are required for tens of thousands of different chemical actions. Because vitamins work on a cellular level, a vitamin toxicity or deficiency can have a number of different potentially lethal repercussions. Plus, the levels required for toxicity or deficiency can vary between types of reptiles, making it even harder to decidewhat your reptile should eat or what a nutrition-related problem might be.

SHOULD YOU SUPPLEMENT?

Deciding what vitamins your reptile should eat and how much is very difficult, even for researchers. Some researchers feel that a diet of natural foods contains adequate amounts of vitamins and minerals, and that oversupplementation can destroy the nutritional balance of the food and can even be hazardous to the animal's health. Other researchers believe that a certain amount of supplementation is needed for several reasons, the most important being that a captive diet is not a natural diet. A snake in the wild does not eat a diet of laboratory-raised mice—it eats wild mice that eat a variety of things, which in turn the snake absorbs when it eats the mouse. A lizard in the wild does not eat a diet of captive-bred and -raised crickets—it eats a variety of small insects.

Before you decide whether or not to add a vitamin supplement to your reptile's food, there is a lot more you need to know. First, you need to understand vitamins and minerals and how they affect your reptile's health. Then, in the following chapters, we will discuss natural foods, live foods, commercial foods and their quality, and then we will discuss supplements themselves.

Plus, you need to understand that one supplement is not good for every reptile. For ease of explanation, we will discuss nutritional needs by dividing reptiles into four basic groups: carnivores (meat eaters), herbivores (plant eaters), insectivores (insect eaters) and omnivores (meat, insect and/or plant eaters). Any exceptions will be discussed separately.

INDIVIDUAL VITAMINS, EXPLAINED

VITAMIN A. Vitamin A is a fat-soluble vitamin that has two forms: carotene and vitamin A. Carotene, which is found in plants, must be converted into vitamin A before it can be used by the body. Preformed vitamin A is the result of that chemical conversion and is found in animal tissues. As a fat-soluble vitamin, excess vitamin A is stored in the liver, in fat tissues, in the lungs, in the kidneys and in the retinas of the eyes.

Vitamin A is an important antioxidant. It helps in the growth and the repair of body tissues and aids in digestion; it also protects mucus membranes, aiding in disease resistance. An immune system enhancing substance, vitamin A is necessary for building strong bones and claws, as well as healthy blood. Vitamin A is also responsible for good eyesight.

A vitamin A deficiency will cause slow or retarded growth, reproductive failure and skin disorders. Secondary infections are also common, as are eye disorders. Because vitamin A is a fat-soluble vitamin, if too much is ingested it can be toxic. Too much vitamin A has also been associated with bone deformities, joint pain and bleeding.

Vitamin A can be found in green leafy vegetables, such as spinach and broccoli, and in yellow and orange vegetables, such as carrots and squash. It is also found in fish oils and animal liver. Most commercial reptile food and supplement manufacturers add vitamin A in one form or another to their commercial food or supplement rather than counting on the ingredients of the food to retain the vitamin during processing.

Chameleons are very sensitive to vitamin A and should not receive a supplement of this vitamin in any form. Carnivorous reptiles—such as mice-eating snakes—may receive adequate amounts in their food; however, a supplement of vitamin A once or twice a week should be fine. Herbivores, insectivores and omnivores could benefit from vitamin A in its beta carotene form.

Box turtles are particularly susceptible to vitamin A deficiencies. Severe hypovitaminosis A (vitamin A deficiency) will show up as swollen eyelids, often stuck shut with a severe discharge from the eyes; blindness and light sensitivity. It will also cause anorexia, diarrhea, sterility, nasal discharge, pneumonia and death. Severe cases must be treated by a veterinarian. Vitamin A deficiencies can be prevented with a good diet that includes a variety of vegetables, meats, insects and a vitamin/calcium supplement twice weekly.

THE B VITAMINS. There are a variety of B vitamins. This group is often called the "vitamin B complex" and includes B1 (thiamine), B2 (riboflavin), B3 (niacin), B5 (pantothenic acid), B6 (pyridoxine), B12 (cyanocobalamin) and B15 (pangamic acid). The B complex also includes biotin, choline, folic acid, inositol and para-aminobenzoic acid (PABA).

The B complex vitamins help provide energy by assisting in the conversion of carbohydrates to glucose, which is the body's fuel. The B vitamins also help the body metabolize protein and fat. These vitamins are needed for normal functioning of the nervous system, for good muscle tone and for healthy skin.

Vitamin B1 (thiamine) works with enzymes to help convert glucose to energy. Also known as the "morale" vitamin, thiamine works with the nervous system and is beneficial to a good mental attitude. Although it is known to improve individual learning capacity in children, this has not yet been proven in animals.

Vitamin B2 (riboflavin) assists in the chemical breakdown of foods. It also works with enzymes to help cells utilize oxygen. Riboflavin is also needed for good vision and healthy skin and nails.

Vitamin B3 (niacin) works with enzymes to metabolize food. It is also effective in improving circulation and reducing cholesterol and is important in maintaining a healthy nervous system.

Vitamin B5 (pantothenic acid) stimulates the adrenal glands, which increases production of adrenal hormones necessary for good health. Vitamin B5 aids digestion, is good for healthy skin and also helps the body withstand stress better.

Vitamin B6 (pyridoxine) is necessary for absorption of vitamin B12. It also helps linoleic acids function better in the reptile's body. Vitamin B6 is also needed for the production of red blood cells and antibodies.

Vitamin B12 (cyanocobalamin) is a cobalt-containing vitamin that works with enzymes to assist in normal DNA synthesis. B12 also works with the nervous system, appetite and food metabolism.

Vitamin B15 (pangamic acid) works to eliminate hypoxia (oxygen insufficiency) in body tissues, especially muscles. B15 also stimulates the glandular systems.

The other B-complex vitamins also serve vital functions. Biotin assists in the oxidation of fatty acids and in the metabolism of other foods. Biotin is also required by the other B vitamins for metabolism.

Choline functions with inositol as a basic ingredient of lecithin.

Folic acid works with B12 and C to metabolize proteins. Folic acid is also necessary for the formation of red blood corpuscles.

All these B vitamins are water soluble; as a result, excess vitamins are excreted instead of being stored in the body. Because the vitamins are not retained, they must be replenished in the diet. The B-complex vitamins can be found in brewer's yeast, liver and whole-grain cereals.

Sulfa drugs and insecticides can destroy these vitamins in the digestive tract. It is also important to remember that most of the B vitamins work together; thus if they are given as a supplement, they should be given together. An excess of one B vitamin could cause a deficiency (or excess) of another.

VITAMIN C. Vitamin C has caused more uproar than any other vitamin available. In humans, vitamin C has been labeled a miracle vitamin because of its ability to fight the common cold. It also serves as an aid in the formation of red blood corpuscles. Vitamin C also fights bacterial infections, maintains collagen, helps to heal wounds and prevents some hemorrhaging. Most important, vitamin C is known to help boost the immune system, fighting and killing viruses.

However, even though vitamin C has so many beneficial properties, many researchers do not feel that reptiles need vitamin C supplements. Most reptiles are able to synthesize vitamin C internally and these researchers feel that any additional vitamin C would be wasted. Some researchers also feel that excess vitamin C can cause a change in the pH (alkalinity-acidity) balance in the kidneys.

However, many other researchers believe otherwise. Alfred Plechner, DVM, stated in his book *Pet Allergies: Remedies for an Epidemic,* "I do believe in vitamin C. It can indeed be helpful in many ways for many animals. Among other things, vitamin C contributes directly to adrenal health and function." Other experts feel that vitamin C can help prevent orthopedic problems in fast-growing reptiles.

As the debate continues, many manufacturers of reptile food are adding vitamin C to their foods, sometimes using ascorbic acid as a preservative. Granted, the amount used to preserve food is small, has a short shelf life and is usually mixed with other substances; however, it is a vitamin C supplement.

At this point, research (and debate) is on-going and until some definitive answers are found, it will be up to the individual reptile owner as to whether or not to supply a vitamin C supplement.

VITAMIN D. Known as the "sunshine vitamin," vitamin D can be acquired from food or it can be absorbed from exposure to the sun. There are three forms of this vitamin: D1, D2, and D3. Mammals use D1 and D2, but reptiles use D3.

Vitamin D is needed for normal calcium-phosphorus metabolism by aiding in the absorption of calcium in the intestinal tract and the assimilation of phosphorus. Vitamin D is needed for normal growth and healthy bones and teeth.

Vitamin D works in conjunction with vitamin A; a deficiency of vitamin A or D can lead to rickets and other bone diseases and deformities. It can also lead to vision problems and kidney disease. Vitamin D is a fat-soluble vitamin and any excess is stored in the liver, brain and skin. Too much can lead to excess calcium and phosphorus in the system, causing calcification in the blood vessels, soft tissues and kidneys.

VITAMIN E. Vitamin E, a fat-soluble vitamin, is actually a group of substances called tocopherols. Found in cold-pressed vegetable oils, raw seeds, nuts and soybeans, tocopherols are antioxidants—substances that oppose oxidation in the reptile's body. Fat oxidation releases free radicals, which can cause extensive damage to the reptile's body. Vitamin E protects both the pituitary and adrenal hormones from oxidation, as well as vitamin B complex and vitamin C.

Vitamin E also assists in the cellular respiration of muscle tissue, including the heart. It also dilates the blood vessels, allowing more blood to reach the heart, and it works to prevent blood clots from forming in blood vessels.

Many manufacturers of reptile food add vitamin E to their foods, often using tocopherols and ascorbic acids as preservatives.

VITAMIN K. Vitamin K is necessary for blood clotting and for normal liver functions. It is a fat-soluble vitamin, and toxicity and abnormal blood clotting can result from too high a dosage.

The best sources of vitamin K are green leafy vegetables, eggs and fish oils.

CHART 3
SOURCES OF VITAMINS

Vitamin	Common Sources*
Vitamin A	Dairy products, leafy green vegetables, fish-liver oil, carrots
Vitamin B complex	Brewer's yeast, whole-grain cereals, liver
Vitamin C	Fruits and vegetables, especially broccoli, cabbage, leafy green vegetables
Vitamin D	Sunshine, dairy products, fish-liver oil
Vitamin E	Cold-pressed vegetable oil, meats, raw nuts and seeds, leafy green vegetables, soybeans
Vitamin K	Kelp, alfalfa, yogurt, egg yolks, fish-liver oil

*Note: These sources are listed not just for direct feeding, but also as sources for nutrients in prepared commercial foods. For example, milk and milk products are *not* appropriate foods to feed directly to reptiles; however, some manufacturers of reptile foods will use whey or other milk products as ingredients to increase the nutritional and biological value of the food.

CHART 4
VITAMIN DEFICIENCIES AND EXCESSES

Vitamin A
Deficiency: Vision problems including blindness and other eye diseases, deficiency disease in box turtles, slow growth, skin problems, diarrhea.
Excess: Nausea, vomiting, diarrhea, bone deformities, bleeding disorders. Dry, flaky skin, skin lesions. Vitamin A toxicity is fatal to many chameleons.
Vitamin B Complex
Deficiency: Fatigue, irritability, nervousness, muscle tremors, anorexia, skin problems.
Excess: Water soluble; when taken as a complex, the excess is usually excreted in the urine. An unusual excess can cause nerve damage or blood or digestive disorders.

Vitamin C (Research ongoing and greatly debated)

Deficiency: Shortness of breath, swollen joints, slow healing, poor immune system response. Skin ruptures or cracks.

Excess: Water soluble; most excess is excreted in the urine. High doses can result in diarrhea.

Vitamin D (specifically D3)

Deficiency: Rickets, bone deformities, poorly developed muscles, nervous disorders, vision problems, metabolic bone disease.

Excess: Increased frequency of urination, nausea, vomiting, muscular weakness, calcification of muscles and organs including the heart and kidneys, renal failure.

Vitamin E

Deficiency: Blood and bleeding disorders, collagen problems, a breakdown in amino acids, reduction in functioning of several hormones, reproductive failure. Muscle tremors, "white muscle disease," muscular dystrophy.

Excess: Generally considered nontoxic; however, it can cause elevated blood pressure.

Vitamin K

Deficiency: Bleeding disorders, reproductive failure.

Excess: Extemely high doses may be toxic.

ALL ABOUT MINERALS

Minerals are present to some extent in the tissues of all living things. Minerals make up parts of your reptile's bones, teeth, muscles, blood and nerves. Minerals help keep the bones strong and the nerves healthy and reactive.

Minerals work with vitamins, with enzymes and with each other. For example, calcium and phosphorus are so closely related and their functions so intertwined that they could actually be called one mineral: calcium-phosphorus. But they are really two minerals that function best together. Many other vitamins and minerals work in much the same way. The B-complex vitamins also need phosphorus for best metabolism; iron needs vitamin C for best absorption and zinc helps vitamin A to be released from the liver. A deficiency of any one mineral can have drastic effects on many systems in the body.

sfigurare to disfigure

sfilare to slip off

sfiorare to touch lightly, skim over

sfoggio display

sfogliato stripped, of its petals

sfogo outlet

sfondare to break down

sforzare to force, strain

sforzo effort, attempt

sfracellare to smash, shatter

sfregiare to disfigure

sfuggire to escape

sgattaiolare to slip away, steal away

sghimbescio: di — obliquely

sgombro clear, free

sgomento dismay, discouragement

sgranare to crumble

sgridare to scold, reprove

sgridata scolding, rebuke, reproof

sguainare to unsheathe

sguardo look, glance, stare

siccità drought, dryness

siccome as

siepe f. hedge

sigaro cigar

significare to mean, signify

significato meaning

signoria Lordship

silenzio silence

silice f. flint, silica

simile like, alike

simmetrico symmetrical

sistema m. system

slancio rush, dash

smarrirsi to lose one's way

smarrito lost, confused

smembrarsi to become dismembered, split up

smettere to stop, leave off

smisurato enormous

smontare to dismount

smorfia grimace

snidare to drive out (from a nest), dislodge

soccorrere to help

soccorso aid, assistance

soffiare to blow

soffitto ceiling

soffocare to suffocate, stifle

soffrire to suffer

soggetto subject

soggezione f. uneasiness; mettere — to make uneasy

soglia threshold

solco furrow

soldato soldier

solido steady, strong, solid

solito accustomed; come al — as usual

solitudine f. solitude; loneliness

sollevare to raise

sollievo relief

somma sum, amount

sommesso subdued, soft

sonagliera collar of bells

sonno sleep

soppesare to weigh in one's hand

sopportare to support, bear

sopprimere to suppress, abolish

sopraggiungere to come up, arrive

soprattutto above all, especially

INDIVIDUAL MINERALS, EXPLAINED

CALCIUM AND PHOSPHORUS. As was just mentioned, calcium and phosphorus are two separate minerals but their functions are so closely intertwined that they could almost be referred to as one combined mineral. Calcium is needed for muscle contraction and neuromuscular transmission and for blood coagulation. Calcium is also vital to some of the body's enzyme reactions.

Because it is present in every cell, phosphorus plays a part in almost every chemical reaction in the body. It is part of the digestion process, and in the production of energy it helps stimulate muscle contractions, including the heart muscle. It is also a vital part of cell reproduction. Working together, the most important function of calcium and phosphorus is to strengthen bones. However, too much phosphorus will inhibit calcium metabolism, resulting in calcium deficiencies.

A calcium deficiency can cause rickets and bone, shell and skeletal disorders and malformations. Moderate deficiencies may cause muscular cramps, joint pain, slow pulse and impaired growth. Calcium-phosphorus imbalances are, unfortunately, quite common in reptiles. The balance of calcium to phosphorus needed for good health varies between types of reptiles. For example, most insects are high in phosphorus, so insect-eating reptiles should eat a calcium supplement that contains no phosphorus. The same applies to carnivores. Herbivores, however, should be get a calcium-phosphorus supplement that contains a ratio of two parts calcium to one part phosphorus (2:1).

Chart 3 "Sources of Vitamins" and Chart 5 "Sources of Minerals" provide additional information, as does Chapter 11, "Supplements."

Meat contains good quantities of phosphorus. Many commercial reptile foods have among their ingredients bone meal or calcium carbonate, either of which is a good source of these nutrients.

CHLORIDE. Chloride is found throughout the body and helps regulate the correct balance of acid and alkali in the blood. Working with salts, chloride maintains pressure in the cells that allows fluids to pass through cell membranes in and out of the cell. It is also needed by the liver to filter wastes from the system.

A deficiency is usually rare, as chloride is found in table salt and most diets contain adequate amounts of salt. However, a deficiency of chloride can cause impaired digestion and poor muscular contraction.

COPPER. Copper assists in the absorption of iron, which is required for hemoglobin synthesis. Copper is also involved in the healing process and helps oxidize vitamin C. Copper is needed to build strong bones, to synthesize phospholipids and to aid in the formation of elastin.

A copper deficiency results in a type of anemia, much like that caused by an iron deficiency. A deficiency can also cause bone or skeletal abnormalities.

Copper is found in liver and fish, as well as whole grains and legumes. The amount of copper found in plant sources can vary depending upon the richness of the mineral in the soil where they were grown.

IODINE. Iodine is a trace mineral that is vital to the proper functioning of the thyroid gland. It plays an important part in regulating the body's energy, in promoting growth and in stimulating the rate of metabolism.

A deficiency of iodine can cause hypothyroidism (an abnormally low secretion of the thyroid hormones), obesity, sluggishness, nervousness and irritability.

Iodine is found in fish, as well as salt with iodine added. Many commercial reptile foods add iodine or potassium iodide as a supplement.

IRON. Iron, working with protein, is present in every living cell in the body. The primary function of iron is to combine with protein and copper to make hemoglobin, which transports oxygen. Iron also works with enzymes to promote protein metabolism. Besides proteins and copper, iron needs calcium to work properly.

A deficiency of iron can cause anemia, the symptoms of which can include difficulty breathing and constipation.

Iron is found in liver, lean meats and fish. Leafy green vegetables, whole grains and legumes also contain iron.

MAGNESIUM. Magnesium helps promote the absorption and metabolism of vitamins and other minerals, including vitamins C and E, calcium, phosphorus, sodium and potassium. Magnesium is also important to protein and carbohydrate metabolism. It aids bone growth, and, in fact, over 70 percent of all magnesium in the body is located in the bones. A deficiency of magnesium will cause cardiac irregularities, muscle twitch and tremors and depression.

Magnesium can be found in leafy green vegetables, raw wheat germ and other whole grains, soybeans, milk, fish and oil-rich nuts and seeds. It is important to keep in mind that cooking, especially at high temperatures, removes magnesium from food, except that food that is processed at very high temperatures and is burned creates ash, of which magnesium is a component.

ZINC. Zinc is a trace element with several important functions; it is vital for the metabolism of a number of vitamins, including the B-complex vitamins. Zinc is also a part of many different enzymes necessary for digestion and metabolism. Zinc is also needed for the healing processes.

Too much calcium in the diet can hamper the absorption of zinc, as can a diet too high in cellulose. A deficiency will show up as a delayed sexual maturity, slow or retarded growth or diabetes.

OTHER MINERALS. There are several other minerals important to your reptile's good health. Selenium works with an enzyme and vitamin E to protect cells. Selenium is found in both meats and cereals, and a deficiency is rare. Manganese, too, works with enzymes and is important to bone growth and reproduction. Cobalt, sulfur and fluorine are other minerals included in your reptile's diet.

MAINTAINING A BALANCE

When discussing your reptile's vitamin and mineral needs, it is important to keep in mind that no one vitamin or mineral functions alone; each has its own function and place in the system, but each is also dependent upon the others. Even if you or your veterinarian decide that your reptile has a deficiency, you must remember to keep the balance of all the nutrients when you supplement your pet's diet.

CHART 5
SOURCES OF MINERALS

Mineral	Common Sources*
Calcium	Meats, bone and bone meal, milk and milk products, nuts, tofu (raw, firm), collard greens, broccoli, beans
Chloride	Salt (sodium chloride), kelp
Copper	Liver, whole-grain products, leafy green vegetables, legumes

CHART 5, CONTINUED

Mineral	Common Sources*
Iodine	Fish, kelp
Iron	Liver, oysters, fish, lean meats, leafy green vegetables, whole grains, legumes, molasses
Magnesium	Green vegetables, raw whole grains, oil-rich seeds and nuts, soybeans, milk
Manganese	Whole grains, eggs, seeds and nuts, green vegetables
Phosphorus	Meat, fish, poultry, eggs, whole grains, seeds and nuts
Potassium	All vegetables, potatoes, bananas, whole grains, sunflower seeds
Selenium	Yeast, organ and muscle meats, fish, whole grains.
Sulfur	Eggs, meat, cheese
Zinc	Whole grains, brewer's yeast, wheat germ, pumpkin seeds

*Note: These food sources are listed not just for direct feeding—such as broccoli for herbivores—but also as potential sources for commercial prepared foods. For example, milk and milk products are *not* good foods to offer as direct foods to reptiles; however, some manufacturers of reptile foods include whey—a milk product—in their foods because of its nutritional and biological food value.

CHART 6
MINERAL DEFICIENCIES AND EXCESSES

Calcium-Phosphorus
Deficiency: Rickets, bone deformities, slow growth, irritability, depression, metabolic bone disease, shell deformities or disease.
Excess: Must have balance between both minerals, according to species.
Chloride
Deficiency: Impaired digestion, poor muscular contractions.
Excess: Adverse reactions suspected but unknown.

Copper

Deficiency: General weakness, impaired respiration, anemia, skeletal abnormalities, skin sores.

Excess: Toxic hepatitis.

Iodine

Deficiency: Enlarged thyroid, dry skin, loss of vigor, slow/poor growth, reproductive failure.

Excess: Unknown.

Iron

Deficiency: Weakness, constipation, anemia.

Excess: Unknown.

Magnesium

Deficiency: Neuromuscular excitability or irritability, tremors, depression.

Excess: Unknown.

Manganese

Deficiency: Slow or retarded growth, reproductive failure, abnormal bone growth, paralysis, ataxia, blindness, deafness.

Excess: Unknown.

Potassium

Deficiency: Respiratory failure, cardiac arrest, nervous disorders, insomnia.

Excess: Unknown.

Selenium

Deficiency: Premature aging, juvenile death, skeletal and cardiac myopathies.

Excess: Hepatitis, nephritis.

Sulfur

Deficiency: Slow or retarded growth, sluggishness, fatigue.

Excess: Unknown.

Zinc

Deficiency: Retarded growth, delayed sexual maturity, diabetes, skin problems.

Excess: Relatively nontoxic but excessive intake may have harmful side effects.

FIVE

FEEDING CARNIVOROUS REPTILES

Many reptiles of different, unrelated species are carnivorous. Carnivores are, by way of definition, meat eaters. "Meat" includes mammals, fish, birds and other reptiles. Most snakes are carnivores, eating fish, rodents, lizards, eggs or even other snakes. Many turtles are carnivores, eating fish, invertebrates and even carrion. Some lizards are carnivores, although most are insectivores or herbivores.*

In the wild, carnivores catch and eat their prey using a variety of hunting techniques. Some hold still and wait for their prey to come to them, and others actively hunt for their prey. In captivity, the prey is usually presented to the reptile and very little—or no—hunting is required. This, along with overfeeding, can lead to obesity, a very common problem in captive reptiles.

The prey that a reptile eats in the wild also varies. Even if a reptile eats only one type of prey—such as lizards or mice—each prey animal will satisfy different nutritional needs. Let's use a typical snake food as an example: mice. One mouse might be eating grain seeds, another might eat pine nuts, another might be nibbling on grass seeds, a fourth mouse might be eating some of everything and a fifth mouse, injured while escaping from an owl, might not have been eating too much of anything. Each of the mice will contribute a different nutritional value to the snake that eats it.

*Lists of recommended foods for the various reptiles are given in Chapter 12.

LIVE FOODS

MICE AND RATS. In captivity, mice commercially raised for sale to reptile owners are usually fed a commercial rodent diet, making them fairly uniform in nutritional value. The uniformity can be very good, providing your reptile a consistently sound diet—or it can lead to nutritional problems if your snake needs more than the mice are providing. Some carnivorous reptiles have suffered nutritional imbalances from eating a diet of obese mice (mice with too much body fat). Other problems have resulted when the mice were fed a less balanced food themselves; the mice pass this imbalance on to the reptile that eats them. Purchasing healthy mice for your reptile is a good investment and it is generally recommended that a vitamin supplement be dusted on the mice (or other live prey) prior to offering the prey to the reptile.

Feeding live prey to your reptile does have some hazards. Mice and rats have sharp teeth and can inflict severe injuries on snakes. For that reason, never leave a mouse or rat in the enclosure with your snake (or other reptile). If the snake isn't hungry and doesn't strike at the mouse after a few minutes, take the mouse out and offer it again later.

RAISING MICE AND RATS FOR YOUR REPTILES

If you have a few reptiles to feed and buying mice seems to be eating a hole in your budget, or if you are concerned about the quality of the mice you're buying, you can raise your own. It will take some money to set up your breeding stock—cages and water tubes aren't cheap—but once you have the supplies, maintenance is relatively inexpensive.

To get set up, you will need cages specifically designed for mice (they're great escape artists!) or aquariums with screen tops. You will need to supply water to the mice or rats. There are several types of hanging waterers for rodents; the type you choose depends upon the type of cage you choose. Don't use a bowl for water. The adult mice will scratch around in their bedding and spill the bowl. An additional risk is that the babies could crawl in and drown.

You will also need bedding for the cages. Pine shaving works very well and is inexpensive. Rabbit food alfalfa pellets also work well and have a pleasant scent. Plan on cleaning the cages weekly.

You will need something to hold food—either bowls or a feeder that hangs on the side of the cage—and you will need food. There are a variety of rodent foods on the market. Keep in mind that your reptiles will be the beneficiaries of whatever you feed the mice, so give them a good quality food.

One male mouse can service (mate with) four female mice. Depending upon the size of your cages, you can house two or three females and one male together. However, don't add a strange mouse to a cage that contains adults with babies—the adults might kill the newcomer. Nursing mother mice will adopt other babies, though, and in fact are wonderful mothers. Many females will put all their babies in one nest and will take turns nursing.

Once established, mice are fairly easy to raise and keep. Excess can often be sold to pet stores or friends with reptiles.

FISH. Some reptiles, especially water turtles, eat fish. A diet composed entirely of fish can lead to some nutritional problems, including a thiamine deficiency. However, reptiles that do eat fish usually eat other things as well, including insects, amphibians and sometimes even other small reptiles.

In captivity, the fish normally fed to reptiles include goldfish and guppies, commonly referred to as "feeder fish." Unfortunately, these fish are not normally well cared for and many times are not fed well. This can translate into nutritional problems in your reptile.

To maintain good nutritional health, it's best to set up a small aquarium with good filtration and plan on keeping these fish for a couple of weeks (or more) prior to feeding your reptile. This way you can discard obviously diseased fish, and you can feed the fish well prior to feeding them to your reptile.

PRE-KILLED LIVE FOODS

The term "pre-killed live food" may sound like an oxymoron, but it refers to live foods—such as mice or rats—that have been humanely killed and then frozen. You can buy them individually or in bulk, keep them in your freezer, thaw them as you need them and offer them to your reptile. This eliminates the need to house and care for live mice or rats, and protects your reptile from injuries that the mouse or rat can inflict. Some reptile owners also have less difficulty feeding pre-killed rodents to their reptile than they would live animals.

Acceptability is sometimes a problem, however. Except for a few reptiles that will eat carrion, like some turtles, most carnivorous reptiles are genetically programmed to catch and eat live prey. Sometimes you can trick your reptile into eating pre-killed food. Thaw the frozen mouse to room temperature and then, using forceps, wiggle it in front of the snake or frog. When the reptile grabs the mouse—let go. Once your reptile eats it a few times, it will learn to accept this as normal prey.

LIVE FOOD SUBSTITUTES

There are also mouse substitutes on the market. Some people are reluctant to feed their reptiles live foods, either for philosophical reasons or for fear that the mouse or rat might bite the reptile, perhaps injuring it. Ocean Nutrition, makers of T-Rex reptile foods, distributes Snake Steak Sausages, made by Dinosaur Nutrition in Great Britain. These sausages are made from whole ground, salmonella-free chickens. The ground meat is packaged in skins, just like breakfast sausages. Included in the meat, inside the skin, is a scent capsule so that to the reptile, this sausage still smells like a mouse. The sausages come in four sizes:

pinkie (baby mouse), fuzzy (slightly older baby), mouse (adult mouse) and young rat.

The problem with food substitutes, such as the sausages, is that many reptiles do not recognize them as food. If a newborn or newly hatched snake is introduced to a sausage as a first food, then acceptability is much higher. However, some adult snakes have been switched over to the sausages with a little work. Again, usually the easiest way is to scent the sausage with a live mouse. Take some cage bedding with some mouse urine and rub it on the sausage; then, using forceps, wiggle the sausage in front of the snake.

I was able to get one of my two Argentine horned frogs to accept the pinkie-size Snake Steak Sausage, but the other frog wouldn't react at all. My rosy boa did eventually accept the substitute after going hungry for a week or two and after I scented the substitute with mouse urine. My ball python acted as if she would fast forever rather than accept the substitute. After offering the sausage several times with no response, I offered a live mouse and she took it right away. Just to see what would happen, I offered the sausage to my Gulf Coast box turtles. The hatchlings ignored it; the juveniles ate it immediately and entirely; the adults ignored it.

FEEDING YOUR CARNIVORE

If your reptile will accept it, offer a variety of live foods. If your snake normally eats small mice, offer a rat pup once in a while. If your frog eats baby mice, offer a goldfish occasionally. Depending, of course, upon your reptile, feed live or pre-killed live foods, and vary this with goldfish, lizards or Snake Steak Sausages. A variety of foods plus a vitamin-mineral supplement will help prevent nutritional problems.

However, keep in mind, too, that many reptiles, especially some snakes, can become very focused on one particular type of prey animal and will not recognize anything else as food. Sometimes you can trick the reptile into eating something else by scenting the new food with a recognized food. For example, if your snake eats lizards and you would like it to accept an occasional mouse, take a lizard and gently rub it on a hairless baby mouse (called a pinkie). This way the mouse will have some lizard scent on it. Using forceps, you can then wiggle the mouse in front of the snake, enticing it to strike.

How you feed your carnivore is just as important as what you feed it. Most reptiles require a temperature of between 80 and 85 degrees to stimulate their appetite, although there are many exceptions. (See "The Importance of Heat" in Chapter 2.) If a reptile is too cool it will not eat, or if it does eat, the food will not digest properly. Therefore, the proper temperature must be maintained prior to feeding and during digestion.

Some reptiles like to hunt (and eat) at night; others during the day. Some like privacy when they're eating; others aren't shy at all. Argentine horned frogs are eating machines and, if maintained at about 75 to 80 degrees during the day, will eat just about anything, any time, with anyone watching. On the other hand some snakes can be very particular. Ball pythons are known to be very poor eaters and can voluntarily fast for months on end. You need to know your particular reptile's needs—both its species' needs and its individual needs.

WHEN NOT TO HAND-FEED

There are some instances when you will not want to feed by hand. If you have a venomous reptile, of course, don't feed by hand. Or if you have snake that will become very large, or is already quite large, like some of the pythons, don't feed by hand. Some snakes will learn to recognize your hand as the giver of food and may strike at your hand, unintentionally causing you some injury.

If you handle your snake a lot, or if you have found that the snake is starting to react to your hand as the source of food, you may want to change your feeding rituals. Some snake owners have stopped feeding their snake in the snake's enclosure, feeding it instead in a brown paper bag or in another enclosure. If you have a small snake, transfer it to a brown paper bag and drop in the live food. Turn over the top of the bag and hold it. Wait until the snake has eaten its prey and then transfer the snake back to its enclosure. A paper bag is not appropriate for a larger snake, but you can do the same thing using a different cage.

SIX

FEEDING INSECTIVOROUS REPTILES

A wide variety of reptiles and amphibians are insectivores (reptiles that eat insects). Anoles in the wild will eat many different kinds of small insects, including aphids, small sowbugs, flies, small worms and crickets. Geckos are masters at catching perching flies or moths and relish the taste of cockroaches. Skinks, chameleons and swifts eat insects. Hatchling turtles eat insects, as do frogs and toads. In the natural balance of things (where there still is such a thing), reptiles are what keep this planet from being overrun by insects.*

Many insects can be fed to your captive reptile. If you have a frog or chameleon that can catch flying insects, houseflies are a tasty treat. If your reptile depends upon stalking or hunting skills, crickets and cockroaches are good hunting. Large earthworms or nightcrawlers are great for bigger insectivores—frogs and turtles—while smaller red worms are good for smaller reptiles.

FINDING INSECTS

HUNTING FOR INSECTS. If you don't spray insecticides or other poisons, you can hunt for insects in your backyard. A net such as those used to catch aquarium fish is great for catching bugs. Go out in your backyard and sweep the net through the lawn, through bushes and shrubs and even through the leaves of your trees. Insects caught in the

---

*Lists of recommended foods for the various reptiles are given in Chapter 12.

net can be transferred to a covered jar for holding. Release any spiders, bees or wasps, and check a local field guide to insects before offering any caterpillars, as many can be poisonous.

Sowbugs and pillbugs can be found in decaying organic material, under boards or leaf litter. These hard-shelled bugs usually roll up when disturbed and can be easily picked up and dropped into a jar.

Earthworms and nightcrawlers can be found under stepping stones, under potted plants outside, in leaf litter or in rotting organic material. Earthworms are more prone to come to the surface after a rain or when the dirt is damp in the evening.

Snails can be found in many southern states and are easily found after a rain. They also hide under yard debris, in leaf litter or in thick plant growth. Slugs are essentially snails without shells and can be found in the same places, although they will also hide in the soil.

If you have small insectivores and have aphids on your plants in the garden, pick a branch from a hibiscus bush or rose bush that has aphids and drop it in your reptile's enclosure. Let your anoles, geckos or swifts have a treat.

RAISING MEALWORMS

Mealworms, scientifically known as *Tenebrio molitor*, are known pests of stored grains. However, they are also well known as a valuable and desirable food source for captive birds, reptiles and amphibians. Mealworms can be bought in small quantities at pet stores or can be purchased in bulk from suppliers and growers (see Appendix II). However, if you feed a number of reptiles and need a quantity of mealworms, they are not difficult to raise.

A five-gallon aquarium with a screen top is a good mealworm enclosure, as the glass sides make it difficult for the worms or adult beetles to crawl out. Wheat or oat bran makes a good culture medium. Pour about three inches of bran in the five-gallon aquarium. Drop in about 100 mealworms (which can be purchased from one of the companies listed in Appendix II or can be bought at your local pet supply store). The mealworms will eat the bran and excrete a sand-like material which will sift to the bottom. Replenish the bran as needed.

In addition, the mealworms will need some moisture. Slice an apple, carrot or potato and lay the slices on top of the bran. The mealworms will eat the fruit or vegetable, leaving the skin, which you can then remove. Do not give the worms dishes or even small containers of water; the water will drown them and cause the bran to mold.

Mealworms have four life stages: egg, larva, pupa and beetle. The mealworm you can buy is the larva stage. As the larva matures, it will turn into a pupa—looking like something out of science fiction—then it will turn into a beetle. Leave the beetles in the culture; they will lay eggs, which will in turn grow into more mealworms.

Mealworms will grow rapidly and move through their life stages if kept at 75 to 80 degrees. If the temperature is much less than that, the mealworms will become lethargic and fail to grow.

INSECTS AT THE PET STORE. A person who doesn't own reptiles would never think of buying insects, except perhaps an angler, who might buy earthworms, mealworms or crickets for bait. However, many insects are available for purchase by reptile owners.

Most pet stores will carry mealworms. Both reptile owners and bird owners buy mealworms, so most stores will keep quite a few on hand. Mealworms usually come prepackaged in plastic containers holding 25, 50 or 100 worms. When kept in the refrigerator, mealworms will stay alive for several weeks.

Most pet stores also carry crickets. Although most crickets sold are for reptiles, many fish keepers will buy crickets for their larger insect-eating fish.

Mealworms and crickets should be fed for a few days prior to feeding them to your reptiles. By feeding the insect well (called gut loading), you are making sure that your reptile is getting better nutrition from the insect. (See the boxes in this chapter on raising mealworms and raising crickets.)

Some pet stores will carry waxworms. Unfortunately, these worms do not keep very well, even in the refrigerator, so many stores will only order the worms when requested. Go ahead and feed waxworms to your reptiles as soon as you purchase them.

INSECTS AT THE BAIT SHOP. Very few pet stores carry earthworms, nightcrawlers or red worms, but you can find these at your local bait shop for anglers. Worms usually come prepackaged in a plastic or Styrofoam container, usually 25, 50 or 100 worms per container.

As with mealworms and crickets, it's a good idea to feed your earthworms and nightcrawlers before feeding them to your reptile. (See the box in this chapter on raising earthworms.)

MAIL-ORDER INSECTS. You can buy just about anything through the mail and that includes food for your reptile. Many companies specialize in insects for reptiles. Rainbow Mealworms, Grubco, Bassett's Cricket Ranch and many others sell insects by mail order, shipped to arrive at your home in tip-top condition, ready to feed your hungry reptile. Again, it's a good idea to feed mealworms, crickets and earthworms prior to feeding them to your reptile.

RAISING YOUR OWN INSECTS

CAN YOU? It's not hard to set up a breeding colony of mealworms, crickets or earthworms, but it does take some material to get started, some time and a little bit of maintenance. Mealworms and crickets take little space, are relatively odorless and reproduce rapidly in the right conditions. Earthworms require more space and sometimes it's hard to keep their culture from smelling. However, if you have room in your yard or basement, earthworms are easy to cultivate.

The advantages of raising your own insects are that you know what the insects have been eating and you always have some on hand. The disadvantages are few and include the time and money required to set up and tend the insects. Another disadvantage is that some people are squeamish about raising bugs. My mother simply does not want to know that I am raising crickets and mealworms in my laundry room; she doesn't understand and doesn't want to understand. Nor does she share my pleasure in seeing a thriving colony of mealworms or listening to the chirping of happily breeding crickets.

If you feed a number of reptiles and would like to try raising your own food, see the boxes in this chapter for guidelines on raising mealworms, crickets and earthworms.

RAISING CRICKETS

In some cultures, a cricket in the house is good luck. To me, the sound of a cricket chirping (which is really the male cricket scraping his wings together) brings back wonderful memories of childhood camping trips.

Crickets are also a good reptile food, and are easily cultured. A five-gallon aquarium with a secure screen top (crickets can jump!) will work well as an enclosure. Put an inch or two of sand on the bottom of the tank, then add some sticks, bark, egg crates or other hiding places for the adults. You can buy adult crickets from your local pet supply store or from one of the suppliers listed in Appendix II.

A jar lid with a piece of wet sponge in it can be used to supply water. Don't give crickets open sources of water—they will drown. Too much moisture will kill them, also.

You can feed them just about anything left over from the kitchen, including bread crusts, apple slices, carrots, oats and pieces of potato. There are also commercial preparations for feeding crickets. Just keep in mind that whatever your crickets eat, your reptiles will in turn eat.

The female crickets will lay their eggs in the sand. The babies are tiny little bugs smaller than the head of a pin (they are called pinheads). You will see them crawling around the cage. They will grow quite rapidly into little miniature crickets; within a month, they will be adults.

FEEDING YOUR INSECTIVORE

There are a couple different schools of thought about how to feed insectivorous reptiles. Some experts say that insects should be offered to the reptile in a small bowl so that the insects cannot escape into the terrarium. When using this method, the reptile owner can see how well the reptile has eaten. If you offered six mealworms in a bowl that the worms could not crawl out of and there are only two mealworms left, you know that the reptile ate four mealworms. Also, when you dust those mealworms with a vitamin-mineral supplement, you know, too, that your reptile has consumed the needed supplement.

The downfall to this method is that some reptiles refuse to eat on command. You may set the bowl of insects out but the reptile may want quiet and security to eat, or darkness, or light. Or it may not be hungry at the moment. Some reptiles, especially many wild-caught reptiles, do not see the bowl as a natural food source and may avoid it.

Some reptile keepers like to establish a more natural terrarium for their reptile, including insects living in the terrarium. This can work well in some instances. If there is bark or other substrate on the terrarium floor, crickets or mealworms can live a complete life cycle in the terrarium, providing food for the reptile inhabitants. Some reptiles are genetically programmed to hunt and many reptile keepers like to watch their reptiles forage for food. After all, it's what they do in the wild.

The downfall to this system is that the reptile keeper has no idea how much the reptile has eaten. Mealworms will burrow into the substrate, as will earthworms. It is also more difficult to ensure that the reptile has eaten any insects dusted with a vitamin-mineral supplement. And last, but certainly not least, crickets can injure reptiles. Crickets may sound charming with their chirping, but they are voracious eaters and can actually start nibbling on your reptile.

It's up to you, as the reptile owner, to decide which method will work best for you and for your reptile. Just keep in mind that your reptile needs a good supply of food that is itself well fed and healthy, and a regular supplement of vitamins and minerals.

RAISING EARTHWORMS

Many different reptiles will eagerly eat earthworms, including many turtles, some lizards, frogs and other amphibians. As an added bonus, earthworms are not difficult to cultivate.

A plastic trash can will serve as a worm farm if you have enough room. If not, a smaller container can be used. Drill or punch some small holes in the plastic—a few at the bottom so that excess moisture can drain out, and a few on the sides to supply some air.

You will want to layer your bedding for the worms. Depending upon the size of your container, put a few inches of sand, dirt, compost or potting soil in the bottom. Follow that with some shredded newspaper, shredded cardboard, leaf mulch or other clippings—but not grass clippings, which are too wet and dense.

Go to your local fishing bait shop and buy some red worms, sometimes called red wigglers—these do well in compost. Add these to your container. Then add some kitchen garbage: apple or potato peelings, salad leftovers, bread crusts or fruit leftovers. *Do not add meat or grease.* Add additional kitchen garbage as the previous is eaten and sprinkle lightly with water once in a while.

Give the worms at least three months to grow; then you can start harvesting. As an additional bonus, the worms' leavings, called vermicompost, is wonderful for your potted plants or garden.

SEVEN

FEEDING OMNIVOROUS REPTILES

The most commonly seen omnivorous reptiles are probably the various box turtles, followed closely by many lizards, tegus, monitors and water turtles. Many turtles, including the popular box turtles, are primarily carnivores as hatchlings but become omnivores as juveniles and adults. Many tegus and monitors will happily eat insects, mammals, fruit and vegetables—a wide variety of foods. Leopard tortoises and sulcata tortoises, which are both primarily herbivores, will occasionally eat carrion, insects, worms, slugs, snails and, in captivity, dog food.

That variety of foods is the hallmark of an omnivore. Omnivores are primarily opportunists, eating whatever is available. Bears, pigs and yes, people, too, are all omnivores, eating whatever happens to be in front of us at the moment we're hungry. Reptile omnivores need that variety of foods to keep good nutritional health. Day geckos do well when they have a variety of small insects to catch as well as pollen, fruit nectar or fruit baby food to eat. Skinks primarily eat fruits and vegetables but on occasion will eat small mammals, insects, small fish and, in captivity, even canned dog food. Box turtles need insects, fruit, berries, vegetables, and, in captivity, small amounts of canned dog food. Plated lizards like small insects, especially waxworms or butterworms, as well as fruit or berries. Bearded dragons like insects and an assortment of vegetables. Nutritional problems are rare when omnivores can have this assortment of foods, with no one food taking precedence, plus a twice-weekly vitamin-mineral supplement.

LIVE FOODS

MICE AND RATS. Mice and rats are very common food items for both omnivores and carnivores. Mice and rats are fairly inexpensive to purchase and are also fairly easy to raise (see "Raising Mice and Rats for Your Reptiles" in Chapter 5). When fed a balanced, nutritious diet, mice and rats will pass that nutrition on to the reptile. However, as was mentioned in Chapter 5, mice and rats fed a poor diet will pass that, too, on to the reptile. Nutritional deficiencies have been found in reptiles fed on mice or rats that were fed a poor diet.

INSECTS AND THEIR RELATIVES. The insects most commonly used to feed reptiles are crickets, mealworms and waxworms. However, other creatures you might normally find in the garden can also be fed to omnivores, including earthworms, sowbugs, snails and slugs.

These creatures, like mice and rats, pass their own nutrition on to the reptile. If the insect is fed a good-quality food, it will pass that on. If the insect is fed just prior to feeding the reptile (called gut-loading) then the reptile actually consumes what the insect just ate. Nutritionally, this can be very beneficial to the reptile.

All these creatures can be very good nutrition when fed in conjunction with other insects and other foods. See Chapter 6 for more information about feeder insects.

PLANT FOODS

FRUITS AND BERRIES. Many omnivores like fruit or berries, especially sweet ones. Day geckos, skinks and plated lizards especially like sweet fruits or nectars. Strawberries, raspberries, grapes, apricots and peaches are all eagerly eaten. Many turtles like melons, strawberries and bananas. Most of these reptiles will also accept baby food fruit.

Avoid citrus fruits—very few reptiles will eat, or can properly digest, citrus fruits. Always core apples and remove the seeds, as these are poisonous. Remove the seeds or stones from grapes, apricots and peaches.

VEGETABLES. Some omnivores will eat a variety of vegetables. Zucchini, squash, sweet potatoes, tomatoes and yams are good foods when cut up, shredded or grated. Some omnivores like chopped dark-green vegetables, but not as enthusiastically as do herbivores.

FLOWERS. Some omnivores enjoy flower blossoms, especially roses and hibiscus. Don't use these blossoms unless you know that they have not been sprayed with an insecticide or fungicide.

GRAIN PRODUCTS. Grain products are not normally fed to omnivorous reptiles as is, but, instead, are used in commercial food preparations. For example, Ocean Nutrition's T-Rex Box Turtle Dry Formula lists as its ingredients some foods that box turtles would be expected to eat, including lamb meal, apples and peaches. However, the ingredients also include oats, corn, corn meal and soy—things that a box turtle would not normally eat.

FEEDING YOUR OMNIVORE

As was mentioned earlier, a variety of foods is important. When offering food to the omnivore, make sure that there is a good balance of foods, depending of course upon the species being fed. Offer the gecko a sweet fruit nectar and a variety of well-fed insects. Offer the red-eared slider some algae as well as some well-fed goldfish and insects. This variety, plus a vitamin-mineral supplement, will help to ensure your omnivore's good nutritional health.

Heat is important to omnivores, just as it is for most other reptiles. Although there are exceptions, most reptiles need a temperature of 78 to 88 degrees to stimulate an interest in eating and to properly digest the food that is eaten. (See "The Importance of Heat" in Chapter 2 for more information on heat and how it affects nutrition.)

Some omnivores will eat anywhere, anytime. Many tortoises are called eating machines by their owners because nothing affects their appetite. However, other reptiles will not eat if all conditions are not right, including heat, light and humidity. Some omnivores like peace and quiet while they eat; others like to eat at night. It's important to find out what conditions your reptile needs and then provide those conditions as much as possible.

EIGHT

FEEDING HERBIVOROUS REPTILES

The most common herbivorous reptile is the green iguana. A popular pet, thousands of iguanas are now being raised on ranches in Central America specifically for importation into and sale in the United States. Other popular herbivores include bearded dragons, uromastix lizards and the terrestial tortoises, including leopard, sulcatta, Russian and gopher tortoises.*

In their native habitat, herbivores eat the plants found in their particular geographical location. California desert tortoises eat cactus pads and blossoms, wild grasses, shrubs and other plants growing in the upper Mojave Desert. Leopard tortoises eat wild grasses, shrubs and cactus, too, but not the same ones as the California desert tortoise. Instead, leopard tortoises eat the plants found in their native South Africa.

However, herbivores are nothing if not adaptable. The same leopard tortoise and desert tortoise will readily eat and thrive on fescue, bermuda grass, bluegrass and rye grass found in a backyard, with supplemental feeding of common vegetables, commercial reptile foods and vitamins and minerals. The majority of reptile herbivores can also thrive on a captive diet as long as it is balanced and varied and is supplemented with vitamins and calcium at least twice a week. The box "Safe, Nutritious Plants for Herbivores" lists a number of different

*Lists of recommended foods for the various reptiles are given in Chapter 12.

plants that can be fed to herbivores. Use this list and the suggestions below to make up a healthy, nutritious, varied diet for your herbivore.

SAFE, NUTRITIOUS PLANTS FOR HERBIVORES

Common Name	Form of Plant
alfalfa	fresh, hay, dried, meal or pellets
apple	fresh—but no core or seeds
banana	peeled fruit
barley	leaves, hay, meal or flour, sprouted seeds
beans	leaves, stems, sprouts
beets	stems, flowers, grated roots
blackberries	fruit
blueberries	fruit
broccoli	heads, grated stems
brussel sprouts	heads
cactus	dethorned pads (leaves), blossoms
carrots	root (chopped or grated)
clover	leaves, blossoms, hay
corn	kernels off the cob
dandelion	leaves, stems, flowers
grapes	fruit
grass	fresh—but without insecticides or fertilizers
hibiscus	flowers, leaves
kale	leaves
millet	leaves, meal or flour, hay
mustard	leaves, flowers
nasturtium	leaves, stems, flowers

okra	fresh or frozen/thawed leaves, flowers
parsley	fresh leaves
pea	pods, fruit
pumpkin	fruit
soybean	leaves, hay, meal or flour
spinach	fresh leaves (do not feed to excess)
squash	blossoms, fruit
strawberries	fruit
sunflower	seeds (unsalted), meal or flour
timothy	hay
tomato	fruit *only*
turnip	leaves, grated root
wheat	sprouted seeds, fresh leaves, bran or flour
zucchini	fruit

PLANT FOODS IN CAPTIVITY

IN YOUR BACKYARD. If you are lucky enough to live in a temperate part of the country where your herbivore can spend some time outside, do so. If your fence is secure enough, let your tortoise graze in your backyard. The grass is more like a natural diet and the sunshine will be wonderful for your tortoise. As an added treat, offer some rose blossoms, hibiscus flowers, some nasturtiums and dandelions as well as a supplemental feeding of commercial herbivore reptile food.

You can also build your iguana an outside cage and let it spend the long summer days outside. Have part of the cage sheltered from sun and weather, but leave part of it open so that your iguana can bask. It will love the sunshine. Offer a dish of vegetables each day, but also cut a branch off a hibiscus bush and let your iguana browse on the blossoms and leaves. There are also commercial iguana foods on the market you may wish to try (see Charts 1 and 2 in Chapter 3).

Even if your herbivore can't go outside, you can harvest plants for feeding inside. As was mentioned, hibiscus leaves and blossoms are enjoyed by most herbivores. Rose blossoms, nasturtium blossoms, dandelion leaves and blossoms, and squash blossoms are all good foods. Flowers are especially good for a reptile that might not be eating well or, as with tortoises, might be coming out of hibernation.

Make sure you know what plants you have in your backyard before you let your herbivore browse, or before you pick a bouquet for your inside herbivore. Many common landscaping plants are poisonous. Check the list in the box "Poisonous Plants" or call your veterinarian, the local nursery or the local poison control hotline.

POISONOUS PLANTS

This is a list of very common poisonous plants, but it is by no means complete. If you have doubts or questions about some plants in your house or yard, call your hospital's poison control center, your veterinarian or your local nursery.
privet

amaryllis	cyclamen
anemone	daffodil
apple (seeds only)	diefenbachia
avocado (leaves, not	dogwood
the fruit)	eggplant (foliage)
azalea	English ivy
belladonna	foxglove
bird of paradise	hemlock
bottlebrush	holly
boxwood	horse chestnut
buttercup	hyacinth
calla lily	impatiens
cherry (seeds)	iris
Christmas cactus	jasmine
common privet	jimson weed
crocus	larkspur
croton	lily of the valley

locoweed	poison sumac
marijuana	pokewood
milk weed	potato (foliage)
mistletoe	privet
morning glory	rhododendron
mushrooms (some	rhubarb
wild ones)	sage
oleander	snapdragon
peach (seeds)	sweetpea
pennyroyal	tomato (foliage)
philodendrons	tulip
poinsettia	vernbena
poison ivy	wisteria
poison oak	yew

IN YOUR REFRIGERATOR. Fresh spinach, kale, romaine lettuce, grated carrots, chopped parsley and grated summer squash are all good foods for herbivores. Tomatoes, sweet potatoes and yams are also good, as are mustard greens, collard greens and swiss chard. In most cases, fresh vegetables should make up the majority of your herbivore's diet. Just keep in mind that a variety of foods is important.

Take care not to feed too many of the plants in the cabbage family—broccoli, cauliflower, brussel sprouts and cabbage—as they can interfere with thyroid function and calcium absorption. Don't eliminate these foods—they are good nutrition—just feed them in small amounts, every other week or so.

Instead of tossing out the leftover salad fixings, leftover dinner vegetables and blemished fruit, save it for your herbivore. As long as there is no salad dressing, butter, cream sauce or mold, it's fine for your iguana or tortoise.

Iceberg lettuce has little to no nutrition but herbivores love it. If you have a finicky eater, or a reptile recovering from injury or disease, you can use this to your reptile's benefit. Use iceberg lettuce to make sure your herbivore eats its vitamins. Chop up the leftover lettuce, sprinkle on the vitamin-calcium supplement and mix it up with the rest of your reptile's meal.

IN YOUR CUPBOARD. Did you forget to pick up some fresh vegetables on your way home from work and your iguana is banging his food dish around? Don't worry. Open a can of mixed vegetables, sprinkle on some vitamins and calcium and offer that. You won't want to use this as a regular diet, but it's perfectly acceptable as an occasional meal.

FRUIT. Strawberries, raspberries, blueberries and grapes are all eagerly accepted by most herbivores. Other good foods include papaya, bananas, melons, apples (with seeds removed) and kiwis. Remove the seed or pit and offer peaches, apricots and nectarines. *Do not offer citrus fruits.*

OTHER FOODS. Pick up a bag of rabbit food at your pet store. Alfalfa pellets make great cage substrate and good food, too. Moisten some pellets and offer them with vegetables. A portion of a piece of whole-grain bread, moistened, can be a good treat to hand-feed your herbivore. Tofu is nutritous and usually accepted quite well.

FEEDING YOUR HERBIVORE

Herbivores have different nutritional needs at different stages of their lives. A young, rapidly growing sulcatta tortoise will need more calcium than will an older, more sedate sulcatta. Sample diets for juvenile and adult herbivores are provided at the end of this chapter. Both these diets should include a reptile vitamin-calcium supplement daily for juveniles and at least twice weekly for adults.

Most herbivores eat during the day. During the heat of summer, some eat in the morning, doze during midday and eat again in the evening. It's important that you offer food when your reptile needs to eat. If your tortoise sleeps during the heat of midday and that's when you offer food, the food could be wilted, spoiled or infested with ants before your tortoise will even pay attention to it.

Make sure your reptile has the proper heat needed for digestion after eating (see Chapter 2). If herbivores get too cool after eating, digestion can stop. This can cause a number of different health problems and can actually be life-threatening.

CHART 7
SAMPLE JUVENILE HERBIVORE DIET

Daily, feed a vitamin-calcium supplement, with calcium-phosphorus at a 2:1 ratio.

Daily Feeding

Calcium-rich green vegetables (40 percent of the daily feeding): alfalfa (hay, chow or pellets, dry or soaked) collard greens, mustard greens, dandelions, spinach greens, cabbage, bok choy, swiss chard, kale, beet greens, green beans, broccoli.

Note: Feed broccoli, kale, spinach, cabbage and bok choy in small amounts as they can chemically interfere with calcium absorption and have been suspected of causing thyroid problems. However, they are good nutrition so don't eliminate them from the diet entirely.

Other vegetables (40 percent of the daily feeding): grated squash, zucchini, bell peppers, sprouts, grated carrots, canned or frozen mixed vegetables, tomatoes, okra, sweet potatoes, clean rose blossoms, clean hibiscus blossoms.

Other foods (20 percent of the daily feeding): mixed-grain bread, natural-bran cereal (no sugar), commercial prepared herbivore food, tofu (raw, firm).

Occasional Feeding (twice a week)

Other foods (these should never amount to more than 20 percent of the daily diet): bananas, apples (with the seeds removed), melons, peaches, strawberries, grapes, fresh or dried figs, papaya, raspberries, blueberries; soaked dry kibble dog food (the high-fiber, diet, reduced-calorie or lite variety); crumbled hardboiled egg.

CHART 8
SAMPLE ADULT HERBIVORE DIET

Daily, feed a vitamin-calcium supplement, with calcium-phosphorus at a 2:1 ratio.

Daily Feeding

Calcium-rich green vegetables (40 percent of daily feeding): alfalfa (hay, chow or pellets) broccoli, cabbage, dandelions, bok choy, swiss chard, kale, beet greens, green beans, spinach and turnip greens.

Note: Feed broccoli, cabbage, bok choy and spinach in small amounts as they can chemically interfere with calcium absorption and are thought to cause thyroid problems when fed in excess. However, these foods are good nutrition so don't eliminate them from the diet entirely.

Other vegetables (50 percent of daily feeding): grated squash, pumpkin, zucchini, sweet potatoes, tomatoes, bell peppers, sprouts, grated carrots, frozen or canned mixed vegetables, peas, lima beans, avocado.

Other foods (10 percent of daily feeding): bananas, grapes, melons, papaya, strawberries, blueberries, raspberries, kiwi, mangoes; commercial prepared herbivore diet.

Occasional Feeding (twice a week or less)

Other foods: Mixed-grain bread, natural-bran cereal (no sugar); soaked dry kibble dog food (the high-fiber, diet, reduced-calorie or lite variety); crumbled hardboiled egg; tofu (raw, firm).

NINE

UNDERSTANDING COMMERCIAL REPTILE FOODS AND LABELS

In previous chapters we discussed your reptile's nutritional needs: proteins for energy, to build healthy cells and for growth; fats for processing vitamins and for healthy skin; carbohydrates and fiber for energy and digestibility and, of course, plenty of clean water. We know that vitamins and minerals often work together and with enzymes for cell function and growth. We even know what foods contain these nutritional building blocks. But how do we know whether or not a commercial food is supplying these needs?

Unfortunately, there is no easy answer. In fact, the nutritional needs of reptiles and the quality of commercial reptile foods are two highly debated subjects, ones that have some researchers fervently defending one position and others arguing exactly the opposite.

DISSECTING THE FOOD LABEL

Every reptile food label must include specific information, which is usually divided into two parts: the principal display panel and the information panel.

The *principal display panel* is very straightforward. It provides the food's:

- brand name (Purina, Ocean Nutrition, Pretty Baby, etc.)
- identity statement (describes the contents: iguana formula, box turtle, etc.)

• designator (identifies species and growth stage: for adults, for juveniles)
• quantity of contents (identifies the weight of the contents)

The *information panel* provides the food's:

• guaranteed analysis (shows the percentages of the food's contents)
• ingredient list (shows ingredients in descending order, by weight)
• feeding instructions (how much to feed your reptile per serving)

The principal display panel is like the name of your town; it identifies where you are but doesn't tell you how to get around. For a "road map" of the food, you need to be able to "read" the stuff on the information panel. Let's review the items found there.

GUARANTEED ANALYSIS

The guaranteed analysis on the information panel of the reptile food label lists the minimum levels of crude protein and fat and the maximum levels of fiber and water. "Crude" refers to the total protein content, not necessarily the amount of protein that is actually digestible. Therefore, the crude protein and fat amounts are simply rough guides. The actual amount depends upon the ingredients and their quality.

The amount of moisture in a food is important, especially when you are comparing foods. A food containing 24 percent protein and 10 percent moisture would have less protein per serving than a food with the same percentage of protein listed on the label but only 6 percent moisture. The box on the next page has a conversion formula so that you can find the dry-matter basis of a food and then discover the actual protein or fat content of that dry matter.

The guaranteed analysis is only a starting place when looking at the label, because it contains so little information. Hill's Pet Products, makers of Science Diet foods, used an advertisement in 1984 that was an excellent demonstration of how the guaranteed analysis could fool the unsuspecting pet food buyer. The ad listed a guaranteed analysis just as it would be found on a can of dog, cat or reptile food, and listed crude protein at 10 percent, fat at 6.5 percent, fiber at 2.4 percent and moisture at 68 percent. This label was very similar to many canned pet foods available. However, the list of ingredients was a shocker! Four pairs of old leather work shoes, one gallon of used crankcase oil, one pail of crushed coal and 68 pounds of water, when analyzed, would equal the guaranteed analysis. Not very nourishing to the animal eating it!

DRY-MATTER-BASIS CONVERSION

The labels of dry, canned, frozen or semi-moist foods look very much alike until you get to the guaranteed analysis, which looks different. The dry food may have a protein percentage of between 26 and 32 percent, while canned foods may have protein percentages of about 8 to 12. Why are they so different? Primarily because of the moisture content, which will be about 65 to 80 percent for canned food and 3 to 10 percent in dry food.

To compare the foods and get a good idea of what their nutritive values really are, you must remove the moisture from the guaranteed analysis and compare both foods as dry matter. Using Brand X and its typical Guaranteed Analysis as an example, here's how you do it:

Brand X Dry Food, Guaranteed Analysis

Protein	20%
Fat	10%
Fiber	10%
Moisture	10%

If a dry food shows that the moisture level is 10 percent, that means the dry solid matter in the food is 90 percent. To find the protein level of this dry matter, divide the 20 percent protein (from the label) by 90 percent dry solids. The answer, 22 percent, is the percentage of protein in the actual dry food.

Let's look at a canned product:

Brand Z Canned Food, Guaranteed Analysis
Protein   5%
Fat   5%
Fiber   10%
Moisture   80%

The conversion for canned food is the same. If the moisture level is 80 percent, this means that the dry solids in this food are 20 percent. To find the protein levels of this food, the 5 percent protein (from the label) is divided by the 20 percent dry solids. The answer, 2.5 percent, is the protein level of the dry solid-matter food.

INGREDIENT LIST

Ingredients are listed in descending order by weight. However, the listings might be misleading. Suppose beef is listed as the first ingredient, causing you to think that it is the primary ingredient. Look again—it may be followed by wheat flour, wheat germ, wheat middlings and so on. The combined wheat products may well total much more than the beef.

The following is a list of some of the ingredients found in commercial reptile foods. Some of these ingredients are for carnivores, some for omnivores, some for herbivores. These descriptions are based on the definitions for animal feed established by the Association of American Feed Control Officials (AAFCO).

MEAT OR MEAT-BASED INGREDIENTS

MEAT is the clean flesh of slaughtered cattle, swine, sheep or goats. It may be only striated skeletal muscle, tongue, diaphragm, heart or esophagus, overlying fat and the portions of skin, sinew, nerve and blood vessels normally found with that flesh.

MEAT BY-PRODUCTS are the clean parts of slaughtered animals—not including meat. It does include lungs, spleen, kidneys, brain, liver, blood, bone, partially defatted low-temperature fatty tissue, and stomachs and intestines freed of their contents. It does not include hair, horns, teeth or hooves.

MEAT MEAL is rendered meal made from animal tissues. It cannot contain blood, hair, hoof, horn, hide trimmings, manure or stomach or rumen contents, except for amounts that may unavoidably be included during processing. It cannot contain any added extraneous materials and may not contain any more than 14 percent indigestible materials, and not more than 11 percent of the crude protein in the meal may be indigestible by the reptile.

MEAT AND BONE MEAL is rendered from meat, including bone, but does not include blood, hair, hoof, horn, hide trimmings, manure, or stomach and rumen contents, except small amounts unavoidably included during processing. It does not include any extraneous materials. Only 14 percent may be indigestible residue and no more than 11 percent of the crude protein may be indigestible.

POULTRY BY-PRODUCTS are clean parts of slaughtered poultry, such as heads, feet and viscera and must not contain feces or foreign matter except in unavoidable trace amounts.

POULTRY BY-PRODUCT MEAL consists of the ground, rendered, clean parts of slaughtered poultry, such as necks, feet, undeveloped eggs and intestines. It does not contain feathers, except those that are unavoidably included during processing.

DEHYDRATED EGGS are whole dried poultry eggs.

ANIMAL BY-PRODUCT MEAL is made by rendering animal tissues that do not fit any of the other ingredient categories. It still cannot contain extra hair, hoof, horn, hide trimmings, manure, stomach or rumen contents, or any extraneous material.

ANIMAL DIGEST is a powder or liquid made by taking clean, undecomposed animal tissue and breaking it down using chemical and/or enzymatic hydrolysis. It does not contain hair, horn, teeth, hooves or feathers, except in unavoidable trace amounts. Digest names must be descriptive of their contents: Chicken digest must be made from chicken, beef from beef and so on.

BEEF TALLOW is fat derived from beef.

FISH MEAL is the clean, dried, ground tissue of undecomposed whole fish or fish cuttings, with or without the oil extracted.

PLANT, GRAIN AND OTHER INGREDIENTS

ALFALFA MEAL is the finely ground product of the alfalfa plant.

DRIED WHEY is whey, dried, and is not less than 11 percent protein or less than 61 percent lactose.

BARLEY is at least 80 percent sound barley, no more than 3 percent heat-damaged kernels, 6 percent foreign material, 20 percent other grains or 10 percent wild oats.

BARLEY FLOUR is the soft, finely ground barley meal obtained from the milling of barley.

BEET PULP is the dried residue from sugar production from sugar beets.

CEREAL FOOD FINES, a by-product of breakfast cereal production, are particles of the foods.

GROUND CORN (also called corn meal or corn chop) is the entire corn kernel ground or chopped. It must contain no more than 4 percent foreign material.

CORN GLUTEN MEAL is the by-product after the manufacture of corn syrup or starch, is the dried residue after the removal of the bran, germ and starch and is high-quality protein.

DRIED KELP is dried seaweed. The maximum percentage of salt and minimum percentage of potassium and iodine must be declared.

LINSEED MEAL is the residue of flaxseed oil production, ground into a meal.

PEANUT HULLS are the outer hull of the peanut shell, ground.

BREWER'S RICE is small fragments of rice kernels that have been separated from larger kernels of milled rice.

BROWN RICE is the unpolished rice left over after the kernels have been removed.

GROUND GRAIN SORGHUM is made by grinding the grains of grain sorghum.

SOYBEAN MEAL is a by-product of the production of soybean oil and is high in protein.

PRESERVATIVES

BHA AND BHT are both preservatives. BHA is butylated hydroxyanisole. BHT is butylated hydroxytoluene. According to the veterinarian Dr. Alfred Plechner, both have been associated with liver damage, fetal abnormalities, metabolic stress and have, as Dr. Plechner states, "a questionable relationship to cancer."

ETHOXYQUIN has been the most highly debated item in commercial pet foods over the last several years. Ethoxyquin is a chemical preservative that has been widely used to prevent spoilage in pet foods. Ethoxyquin was approved by the U.S. Food and Drug Administration (FDA) in 1956. It has been alleged that ethoxyquin has caused cancer, liver, kidney and thyroid dysfunctions, reproductive failure and more.

An independent testing laboratory is conducting a new test on ethoxyquin. This test is following testing protocols approved by the FDA, which will evaluate the study prior to the release of the results to the public.

Many pet food manufacturers still use ethoxyquin (see the box on the next page about preservatives); however, because of public concern, many manufacturers have switched to other means of preserving their foods.

SODIUM NITRATE is used both as a food coloring (red) and as a preservative. When used in food, sodium nitrate can produce carcinogenic substances called nitrosamines. Accidental ingestion of sodium nitrate by people can be fatal.

TOCOPHEROLS (vitamins C and E) are naturally occurring compounds used as natural preservatives. Tocopherols function as antioxidants, preventing the oxidation of fatty acids, vitamins and some other nutrients. These are being used more frequently as preservatives because many reptile owners are more concerned about chemical preservatives; however, tocopherols have a very short shelf life, especially once the bag of food has been opened.

PRESERVATIVES USED IN COMMERCIAL REPTILE FOODS

Kaytee Adult Iguana Daily Diet: propionic acid and ethoxyquin

Land Turtle and Tortoise Daily Diet: none

Nutri Grow Iguana Growth and Maintenance Formulas: ascorbic acid

Ocean Nutrition T-Rex Box Turtle Dry Formula: none

Tortoise Dry Formula: none

Iguana Adult Fruit & Flower Formula: propionic acid and BHT

Iguana Adult Vegi Formula: none

Iguana Juvenile Vegi Formula: none

Iguana Juvenile Fruit & Flower Formula: none

Pretty Pets Adult Iguana Food: propionic acid

Tetra ReptoMin Floating Food Sticks: ethoxyquin

Tetra Terrafauna Reed's Iguana and Tortoise Food: ethoxyquin

Zoo Med Zoo Menu Box Turtle/Tortoise Food: ascorbic acid

Zoo Med All Natural Iguana Food: tocopherols and ascorbic acid

Zoo Med Zoo Menu Aquatic Turtle Food: ethoxyquin

WHAT ARE THOSE OTHER INGREDIENTS?

The National Research Council believes that adequate amounts of needed nutrients can be obtained by eating a well-balanced diet consisting of a selection of the proper ingredients. However, Lavon J. Dunne, author of the *Nutrition Almanac* (Nutrition Search, Inc.,

McGraw Hill, 1990), states that there is much more to nutrition than that. "Other factors affecting adequate nutrition are insufficient soil nutrient levels resulting in nutrient-deficient foods. Food processing and storage deplete foodstuffs of valuable vitamins and minerals." Dunne continues by saying that many nutrients are lost or depleted during cooking, especially at high temperatures.

To ensure that their foods are complete and balanced nutritionally, many reptile food manufacturers add vitamins and minerals to the food during processing. Sometimes these are added in a natural form, as an ingredient. For example, yeast is added to many foods because it is an excellent source of selenium, chromium, iron, magnesium, manganese and many other needed nutrients.

Natural vitamins can be separated from their natural source, either plant or animal, and used as an additive. The vitamin (or mineral) is considered natural as long as there has been no change to its basic molecular structure.

Vitamins or minerals can also be added to the food in a synthetic form, a manufactured form. Synthetic vitamins and minerals usually contain a salt such as sulfate, nitrate or chloride, which helps stabilize the nutrient. Most researchers feel that the body absorbs synthetic vitamins as well as it does natural vitamins, with very little difference in metabolism, except for vitamin E, which works much better in natural form.

CHEMICAL NAMES AND WHAT THEY ARE

Many of the chemical names listed on reptile food labels are the chemical names of natural or synthetic vitamins and minerals added to food during processing.

ASCORBIC ACID is a synthetic form of vitamin C.

BIOTIN is a natural B-complex vitamin.

CALCIUM CARBONATE is a natural form of calcium.

CALCIUM PANTOTHENATE is a high-potency, synthetic source of vitamin B5.

CALCIUM OXIDE is a natural form of calcium.

CALCIUM PHOSPHATE is a calcium salt found in or derived from bones or bone meal.

CHLORIDE OR CHLORINE is an essential mineral, usually found in compound form with sodium or potassium.

CHOLINE is a B-complex vitamin found in eggs, liver and soy.

CHOLINE CHLORIDE is a high-potency, synthetic source of choline.

COBALT is a trace element, an essential mineral and an intregal part of vitamin B12.

COPPER is a trace element, an essential mineral that can be toxic in excess.

COPPER CARBONATE is a natural form of copper.

COPPER GLUCONATE is a synthetic form of copper.

COPPER SULFATE is a synthetic source of copper.

FERROUS SULFATE is a synthetic, high-potency source of iron.

FOLIC ACID is a B-complex vitamin found in yeast or liver.

INOSITOL is a B-complex vitamin.

IRON OXIDE is a natural source of iron.

MAGNESIUM OXIDE is a natural source of magnesium.

MENADIONE SODIUM BISULFITE COMPLEX is a source of vitamin K.

PANGAMIC ACID is vitamin B15.

PANTOTHENIC ACID is vitamin B5, a coenzyme.

POTASSIUM CHLORIDE is a high-potency, synthetic source of potassium.

POTASSIUM CITRATE is a natural form of potassium.

PYRIDOXINE HYDROCHLORIDE is a synthetic source of vitamin B6.

RIBOFLAVIN is a synthetic source of vitamin B2.

SELENIUM is an essential mineral.

SODIUM CHLORIDE is a synthetic form of salt, table salt.

SODIUM SELENITE is a synthetic form of the essential mineral selenium.

TAURINE is an amino acid.

THIAMINE HYDROCHLORIDE is a synthetic source of vitamin B1, thiamine.

THIAMINE MONONITRATE is a synthetic source of vitamin B1.

ZINC CARBONATE is a source of the mineral zinc.

ZINC OXIDE is a natural form of the mineral zinc.

ZINC SULFATE is a synthetic form of the mineral zinc.

ARTIFICIAL COLORING

Many of the artificial colorings used in pet foods have been associated with potential problems. FD & C Red No. 40 is a possible carcinogen but is widely used to keep meat looking fresh. Blue No. 2 is thought to increase some animals' sensitivities to viruses. Another color that is commonly used but has not been fully tested is Yellow No. 5. Red No. 2 and Violet No. 1 were banned by the FDA in the mid-1970s as possible carcinogens, but prior to that were widely used in pet foods.

THERE'S MORE!

SUGAR is not an ingredient most people would expect to find in reptile food, but some reptile foods do contain sugar. The sugar adds palatability and moistness and aids in prevention of bacterial contamination, but this amount of sugar is definitely not needed by most reptiles and can stress the pancreas and adrenal glands, causing diabetes or other problems. Completely devoid of protein, vitamins and minerals, sugar is, literally, empty calories.

SALT is added to many foods as a meat preservative. Too much salt can irritate the digestive system and can cause a mineral imbalance because the salt itself can upset the calcium-potassium balance.

REMEMBER QUALITY

The presence of some or all of the above-listed ingredients, which are the most commonly used reptile food ingredients, or an assortment of these ingredients, doesn't necessarily mean that your reptile is going to be well nourished. The ingredients must be in the right combinations and of good quality, both before and after processing.

BIOLOGICAL VALUE. The biological value of the ingredients is one of the keys to good nutrition. The biological value of a food is the measurement of the amino acid completeness of the proteins contained by the food. Eggs are considered a wonderful source of protein because they contain all the essential amino acids. Therefore, eggs have a biological value of 100 percent. Fish meal is 92 percent and beef is 78 percent, as is milk. Wheat has a biological value of 60 percent, wheat gluten is 40 percent and corn is 54 percent. Neither wheat nor corn would be an adequate diet alone, but fed together with one or two meat-based proteins capable of supplying the missing amino acids, they could supply an adequate diet.

For example, Zoo Med's Iguana food, juvenile formula, lists as the first ingredients alfalfa, wheat bran, soybean meal, collard greens, mustard greens, kale and spirulina. These, along with the other ingredients, supply a diverse number of protein sources, which makes the biological value of the food high, for iguanas.

DIGESTIBILITY OF FOOD. Digestibility refers to the quantity of the food that is actually absorbed by the reptile's system. The more food that is actually metabolized, the higher the digestibility figure. During feeding trials, the reptiles' feces are collected and analyzed as to the undigested residues of the food eaten.

Dr. Steve Hannah, a nutrition scientist with Purina, says, "Digestibility is determined by the amount of food consumed by the animal, minus the amount of undigested or unabsorbed food in the stool."

High digestibility indicates that the nutrients in a given food are available to be used by the animal. Consideration is given, too, to the type of animal and the normal digestive processes for that type of reptile.

QUALITY BEFORE PROCESSING. Understanding the definition of an ingredient is not enough—a short description doesn't tell us exactly how good that ingredient is. Many grains grown in poor soil will lack needed vitamins and minerals, and, unfortunately, this is happening quite often in the United States. Grains and vegetables can be polluted with pesticides of various kinds and fertilizer residues.

Ingredients can also be soiled with molds, mildews and fungus. The quality of meat can also be suspect—we have all heard stories of finding bits of hair and other unsavory additives in our hamburger—and the quality of meats used for reptile foods is much less. The U.S. Department of Agriculture (USDA) has said that there is no mandatory federal inspection of ingredients used in pet food manufacturing. However, some states do inspect manufacturing plants, especially those producing canned foods.

In the majority of the states it is legal (and common practice) for pet food manufacturers to use what is commonly called 4-D meat sources—animals that are dead, dying, diseased or disabled when they arrive at the slaughterhouse. Dr. P. F. McGargle, a veterinarian and a former federal meat inspector, believes that feeding slaughterhouse wastes to pet animals increases their chances of getting cancer and other degenerative diseases. He said, "Those wastes include moldy, rancid or spoiled processed meats, as well as tissues too severely riddled with cancer to be eaten by people."

Richard H. Pitcairn, DVM, Ph.D., and Susan Hubble Pitcairn, authors of *Natural Health for Dogs and Cats,* remind us of another group of additives that has been left off the pet food packages—hormones, insecticides and other chemicals. The majority of livestock used for food production are loaded with growth hormones, pesticides, antibiotics and other chemicals. Meat from fetal tissues of pregnant cows is naturally high in hormones and high cooking temperatures do not deactivate these hormones.

QUALITY AFTER PROCESSING. Many nutrients—especially enzymes and some vitamins and minerals—can be damaged by the high temperatures used in processing pet foods. If the nutrients are in the raw foods but are damaged during processing, they are obviously not going to help your pet.

NAME, ADDRESS AND PHONE NUMBER OF THE MANUFACTURER

This is provided on the label so that you can contact the manufacturer if you have any questions about the product. Make sure that you have the bag, can or box of food in front of you when you call as the representative will ask for the product code.

IN CLOSING

Reptile food labels do provide quite a bit of information, and learning how to decipher them can take some time. Don't try to do it when you're shopping, in a hurry, standing in the aisle, looking at all the foods available. Instead, study the labels at your leisure. You might even buy a variety of foods (or ask if samples are available) so that you can compare the labels at home and, more important, so that you can see if your reptile is even attracted to the food.

As you study, keep in mind that there is also much information not given on the label, such as the quality of the ingredients used. As we know, that information can be very difficult to come by, but feel free to call the company and ask to speak to someone who can answer your questions. In the end, make your decision based upon your understanding of the label, the recommendation of experts (including your veterinarian), your opinion as to the philosophy and reputation of the company and the price of the food itself.

TEN

CHOOSING THE RIGHT COMMERCIAL FOOD

There are quite a few different reptile foods available to pet owners, with more appearing each year. There are canned foods, dry foods, flakes, floating foods, semi-moist and frozen foods. Some foods are incredibly expensive and others are very cheap. There are very nutritious, complete foods made with ingredients approved for human use and other foods of dubious nutritional value with very questionable ingredients. Some foods are nationally advertised while others are known in small geographical areas and promoted by word of mouth.

How can you sift through this cornucopia of foods and narrow the field down to one? Again, knowledge is the key—knowledge of the foods, what they are and what the terms mean.

FORMS OF FOODS, AND THEIR PROS AND CONS
Most reptile foods come in one of five different forms:

- dry kibble, pellets or dry flakes
- canned
- semi-moist
- frozen
- live

DRY KIBBLE, PELLET AND FLAKED FOOD. One of the most common forms of reptile food is dry food. Dry food usually has a moisture content of 10 to 12 percent or less and contains grains and grain products, vegetables and other ingredients, including meats. Most dry foods are made using an extruder, a machine that can cook the food at a high temperature for a very short period of time. The shelf life is normally three to six months, depending upon the method of preservation used.

Pros: Dry kibble reptile foods have a good shelf life, are easy to serve and store, and are the most reasonable in price. There is little annoying odor—in fact most of the foods have a very pleasing odor. Many omnivorous and herbivorous reptiles will readily accept an appropriate dry food if it has first been soaked in water.

Dry flake foods are typically fed to amphibians or water turtles and are usually dropped in the water where they float until eaten. Some reptiles will easily switch from live foods to flakes; others are not so eager.

Cons: One drawback to dry food is that reptiles used to eating natural foods will sometimes resist a change to dry food. For this reason, some owners spice up the dry food by adding chopped vegetables or fruits to it—foods that the reptile is used to eating. Another drawback is that dry foods often contain a number of different artificial colorings, flavorings and preservatives.

CANNED FOODS. There are several canned reptile foods on the market. Most are aimed at a specific target reptile. Zoo Med offers a number of different foods, including a canned iguana food and a canned tegu and monitor food. Canned foods have a higher moisture content than do dry foods, usually 70 to 80 percent. Although most people expect canned pet foods to be meat or meat based, canned foods can and do contain ingredients other than meat.

Pros: Canned foods are very palatable to most of the target reptiles. Canned foods also have a very long shelf life.

Cons: Canned foods are more expensive than dry foods and the content of a can does not go as far, nutritionally, as does dry food. Canned foods sometimes have a less than pleasing odor (to the reptile owner, anyway).

FROZEN FOODS. Frozen reptile foods come in many different forms, from frozen worm cubes (like fish foods) to frozen fish, frozen mice or mice substitutes. The process of freezing provides reptile food manufacturers with a number of different options regarding foods.

Frozen foods are usually high in moisture content, sometimes as much as 50 to 70 percent. These foods can also contain ingredients other than fish or meat, depending upon the food, although most frozen foods are meats of some kind. The shelf life of these foods varies, depending upon the processing and the ingredients. An expiration date is usually on the package. Cost also varies, depending upon the ingredients and the brand.

Pros: When thawed, frozen foods are very palatable and most reptiles eagerly eat the food, once introduced to it. Unused portions should remain in the freezer, making them less likely to spoil.

Cons: Unfortunately, many pet supply stores do not have freezers and thus cannot carry these foods. Other pet stores carry very limited amounts or varieties. Because it must be thawed ahead of time, more thought and planning is required on your part to feed the reptile than with many other food forms. Sometimes the reptile must be taught to accept a frozen type of food, especially if you are trying to switch from live foods to a frozen food.

Semi-Moist Foods. Semi-moist foods are somewhere between canned and dry foods in moisture content. Most have a moisture content of about 30 percent. Many of these foods list meat as one of the first five ingredients, but they also contain a variety of other ingredients, some including sugar or sugar products.

Pros: These foods are usually easily accepted by the reptile, especially the tortoise and box turtle foods.

Cons: As was previously mentioned, semi-moist foods often contain great amounts of sugar, which is not a good source of nutrition. Semi-moist foods are also more expensive than dry foods and somtimes contain a number of artificial colors, flavorings and preservatives.

Live Foods. Live foods are discussed in detail in Chapters 5 and 6. Live foods are usually insects (crickets, mealworms, waxworms, earthworms) or rodents (mice, rats, rabbits). Sometimes live foods, especially rodents, are killed prior to feeding to the reptile. Live foods are natural foods for many reptiles. Although some reptiles will readily change over to frozen foods or commercially prepared food substitutes, some reptiles will not accept anything but a natural live food.

Pros: Live foods are more like what the reptile would eat in the wild. If the live food is "gut loaded"—pre-fed nutritious food—the reptile owner is more assured that the reptile is eating well.

Cons: Live foods often require more work for the reptile owner: Feeding them involves finding, ordering or purchasing the food; keeping the food alive until feeding time and making sure the live food is properly fed and cared for. Then, too, many reptile owners have reptiles because they love animals and do not like feeding live foods. And last, live foods can sometimes inflict injury to reptiles or can carry disease, parasites or toxins (insecticides or pesticides).

MIXING FOODS

Many reptile owners mix foods on a regular basis. Some reptile owners want to provide a varied diet, for example, mixing chopped vegetables, a few fruits and some soaked dry kibble food for an iguana or tortoise. Box turtles might be fed some soaked, dry kibble, some canned dog food, a few berries and some earthworms.

Many experts feel that a mixture might be the best answer for many reptiles because the variety can better ensure a higher biological value of the total food consumption. However, when putting together the diet of varied foods, care must be taken to ensure that all the foods are high quality and are appropriate to that specific reptile.

CHART 9
IGUANA FOODS TASTE TESTS

To compare the palatability and acceptance of some commonly available iguana foods, I used my two iguanas. Both are used to trying a variety of foods and neither is a finicky eater.

To conduct the test, I spread the foods out in front of the iguana, at equal distances, and noted the reptile's reactions.

These are not scientific tests: I used only my two reptiles, there were no controls of any kind and I performed the tests only once with each iguana. However, it is interesting to note the iguanas' reactions to the foods.

Test 1

Iguana used: Cannible, a juvenile female, about 30 inches from nose to tip of tail.

Foods offered:
      Ocean Nutrition T-Rex Iguana Juvenile Fruit
      Ocean Nutrition T-Rex Iguana Juvenile Vegi

Tetra Reed's Iguana Food

Zoo Med All Natural Iguana Juvenile Food

Results: Cannible sniffed in the direction of each of the foods before moving. She took a bite of the T-Rex Fruit formula, then a bite of the T-Rex Vegi formula, then settled down to eat the Zoo Med All Natural formula.

Test 2

Iguana used: Conan, a seven-year-old male, ten pounds in weight, over five feet long.

Foods offered:

Kaytee Adult Iguana

Ocean Nutrition T-Rex Adult Fruit & Flower

Ocean Nutrition T-Rex Adult Vegi Formula

Pretty Pets Adult Iguana

Zoo Med All Natural Iguana Adult Formula

Results: Conan seemed momentarily overwhelmed by the foods in front of him but recovered quickly. This iguana has a great appetite! Conan went directly to the T-Rex Fruit & Flower and ate the entire sample before moving on. Second to be eaten was the Pretty Pets food and third was the T-Rex Vegi formula.

CHART 10
TORTOISE FOODS TASTE TESTS

I wanted to test the acceptibility and palatability of some of the commonly available commercial reptile foods. However, understand that these tests are unscientific: I used only my reptiles and I used no controls. In addition, I did each test only once. However, the results are interesting and show each animal's response to the foods.

To test the foods, I placed a variety of foods in front of each animal, at equal distances, and watched the results.

Test 1

Tortoise used: Pearl, a thirty-pound leopard tortoise.

Foods offered:

Kaytee Land Turtle and Tortoise Food

Nutri Grow Herbisaur

Ocean Nutrition T-Rex Dry Tortoise Formula

Pretty Pets Small Tortoise Food

Zoo Med Box Turtle and Tortoise Food

Results: Pearl went directly to the T-Rex food, ate it completely and then ate the Pretty Pets food. She took a bite of the Kaytee food and moved on to the Zoo Med food, took a bite and then tried the Nutri Grow food.

Test 2

Tortoise used: Harley, a juvenile five-pound sulcatta.

Foods offered: Same as those in Test 1.

Results: Harley started with the Pretty Pets food and, after eating the entire sample, ate the T-Rex food, the Kaytee food, followed by the Nutri Grow food.

Test 3

Tortoise used: Gem, an adult Russian tortoise.

Foods offered: Same as those in Test 1.

Results: Gem went directly to the T-Rex food, ate it all, then started to taste all the others, one bite at a time.

CHART 11
BOX TURTLE FOODS TASTE TESTS

These tests were to test the palatability and acceptability of some of the commonly available turtle foods. I used my own turtles to test the foods. I tested the foods by placing samples of each of the listed foods equal distances in front of the turtle. I then watched to see what happened.

These tests are unscientific as I did each test only once, had no controls and used only my own pets. The results were very interesting.

Test 1

Turtle used: Onyx, a very old, long-term-captive Gulf Coast box turtle.

Foods offered:

Kaytee Land Turtle and Tortoise Daily Diet

Nutri Grow Carnisaur

Nutri Grow Omnisaur

Ocean Nutrition T-Rex Box Turtle Dry Formula

Pretty Pets Box Turtle Food

Zoo Med Zoo Menu Box Turtle/Tortoise Food

Results: Onyx much prefers live foods—mealworms, snails, slugs and earthworms—but when they weren't offered during this test, she tried the prepared foods. She went directly to the Nutri Grow Carnisaur and took several bites, wandered over to the Omnisaur and sniffed it. She then crawled through the Kaytee food, mashed down the Zoo Med food and finally ate some of the T-Rex food. If there were any favorites, they seemed to be the Carnisaur and the T-Rex box turtle food.

Test 2

Turtle used: Topaz, an adult long-term-captive eastern box turtle.

Foods offered: Same as those in Test 1.

Results: Topaz ate the Nutri Grow Carnisaur, finished this sample, then went directly to the T-Rex sample and ate that as well. She then crawled off, apparently finished with her meal.

Test 3

Turtle used: Star, a three-year-old captive-bred Gulf Coast box turtle.

Foods offered: Same as those in Test 1.

Results: Star sniffed most of the foods before sampling anything, but eventually settled down to eat the Pretty Pets Box Turtle food.

Test 4

Turtle used: A clutch of eight four-month-old Gulf Coast box turtle hatchlings.

Foods offered: Same as those in Test 1.

Results: The hatchlings hit all the foods, eating as if they were starved (I know better!). All the foods were eaten equally well.

ELEVEN

SUPPLEMENTS: SHOULD YOU OR SHOULDN'T YOU?

Most nutritionists and veterinarians consider a supplement to be anything that is added to the reptile's diet on a regular basis. Should you use supplements? As with so many aspects of reptile nutrition, the experts' opinions vary. Some say that a good-quality food (or diet) is all the reptile needs. Many of the commercial reptile food manufacturers state that their food is "complete and balanced" and needs no supplementation.

However, many other experts say that even a "complete and balanced" reptile food is not always enough; that it doesn't take into consideration each species' needs, each individual reptile's needs or the actual quality and digestibility of the food or diet.

Dr. Clarence Hardin, the director of the California Mobile Veterinary Service and a known preventive medicine vet, is in favor of dietary supplements. He says, "Today's pets face a number of critical health dangers, including air and water pollution and substandard, chemically laden foods. Often traditional nutrition and medicine is not enough."

DECIDING TO SUPPLEMENT

Deciding what supplements to add to the reptile's diet is often difficult. Some reptile owners might see an advertisement for a new product that is supposed to be on the cutting edge of nutrition and will decide to try it, while other reptile owners might hear or read about a supplement that is supposed to accomplish something specific, such as produce healthy bones, and they will decide to try it. Other reptile owners do a lot of research, searching out exactly the right nutrients for their reptile.

As long as the supplement itself is appropriate to the reptile species and is not harmful to the reptile, and the amount given is appropriate to the reptile's size, condition and general health, the only real danger in supplementing a diet is that the supplement may unbalance a previously balanced, complete food or diet.

When you give supplements, it is important that you watch closely the reptile's overall condition and health. If there appears to be any kind of allergic reaction, stop the supplement and call your veterinarian. If there is any detrimental change in the reptile's condition or health, again, stop the supplement and talk to your veterinarian.

COMMERCIALLY AVAILABLE SUPPLEMENTS

VITAMIN-MINERAL SUPPLEMENTS. There are probably as many vitamin-mineral supplements available for reptiles as there are for people. There are complete vitamin-mineral preparations, vitamin-calcium supplements, calcium-phosphorus or calcium-only supplements, and there are supplements containing one specific vitamin or mineral.

When you are supplementing a homemade diet, such as mixed vegetables for a herbivore, it's fairly easy to determine what your reptile should get as a supplement—a vitamin-calcium supplement with a calcium:phosphorus ratio of 2:1. However, when supplementing a commercial food that is supposed to be complete and balanced, it's important to know what vitamins and minerals the food contains and in what amounts. With many vitamins and minerals, too much is just as dangerous as too little. If you are in doubt for what your reptile is getting from its food, call the manufacturer and ask.

Sometimes individual vitamins or minerals are recommended for a specific purpose. Chapter 4 discusses vitamin and mineral deficiencies (as well as excesses) and can serve as a guideline for what you may want to supplement.

CALCIUM AND PHOSPHORUS. Calcium-phosphorus imbalances cause the most common nutritional disorders that veterinarians see in reptiles. These imbalances can cause "soft shell" syndrome in turtles and tortoises and metabolic bone disease in iguanas, as well as many other equally serious health problems. Fortunately, proper husbandry practices (temperature, light and humidity) as well as proper nutrition can prevent the vast majority of these disorders.

A.C. Highfield, the author of *Keeping and Breeding Tortoises in Captivity*, recommends that herbivorous tortoises be fed a calcium: phosphorus ratio of 2:1 for rapidly growing juveniles and a ratio of at least 1.25:1 for adults. Ray Hunziker, the author of *Horned Frogs* (TFH, 1994), recommends a supplement with a calcium:phosphorus ratio of 2:1 for horned frogs.

If your reptile is eating a good, balanced diet appropriate to its species, adding a calcium-phosphorus supplement that is also in balance will not disturb the biological value of the diet itself. Supplements alone will not cure nutritional problems—they are, instead, one piece of the nutritional puzzle.

ENZYME FORMULAS. Enzyme formulas are designed to enhance or replace naturally occurring enzymes. These are usually added to aid digestion. Most enzyme supplements are derived from plant sources, such as papain or bromelain. Because enzymes work in conjunction with other body processes, enzyme supplements should not be added to any reptile's diet without first consulting a veterinarian experienced in reptile nutrition.

Enzyme supplements can be especially beneficial to a herbivore on a high-fiber diet. Fiber is known to interfere with zinc absorption in the intestinal tract, and additional enzymes can free up those and other nutrients in the fiber, making them more available for metabolism.

One popular formula, Prozyme, is advertised as "enhancing the bioavailability of all pet foods." It is supposed to work directly on the food by replacing the natural enzymes lost during processing.

FOOD SUPPLEMENTS. A few supplements are available that are made from foods rather than simpler food forms, such as vitamins, minerals, fatty acids or enzymes. Most of these supplements are designed to provide more complete nutrition for pets, aiding what might otherwise be a less-than-complete diet.

#1 All Systems, a company known for its pet grooming products, has produced a supplement called Vital Energy. Made from flax seed, molasses, yeast, rice bran, liver, alfalfa and a number of other quality ingredients, Vital Energy contains antioxidants, phytochemicals, enzymes, amino acids, trace minerals and vitamins. Vital Energy is itself a balanced food, eliminating the concern of oversupplementation.

Vital Energy has been used by some tortoise rescuers (people who take in tortoises). Some of these tortoises were severely malnourished or had been injured in some way or were diseased. The tortoises were fed a normal diet appropriate to their species with Vital Energy sprinkled on top and were allowed to graze on clean grass. This was an unscientific study or experiment since all the tortoises came to the rescue center in different states of health and received different veterinary care. There were no control animals, either. However, the majority of the tortoises ate the supplement willingly and most were returned to good health and eventually adopted out to new homes.

IN CLOSING

Adding a supplement to your reptile's food is a personal decision that should not be undertaken lightly. Too much supplementation can upset a previously balanced and complete diet. For example, as has been discussed in detail previously, a calcium-phosphorus imbalance can result in myriad potentially lethal health problems.

However, supplements added to the diet wisely can benefit your reptile greatly. The key to using supplements is to do so intelligently, researching the supplement and the food your reptile eats. If you have any doubts, talk to the reptile food manufacturer, and if the supplement you are adding is a commercially manufactured supplement, talk to that company's representative as well. If you see any detrimental changes in your reptile's health, of course stop the supplement immediately and call your veterinarian.

CHART 12
COMMERCIAL VITAMIN AND MINERAL SUPPLEMENTS

Sprays

ESU Reptile Products Carnivore Calcium
   For carnivorous and omnivorous reptiles
   Phosphorus-free calcium and vitamin D3
ESU Reptile Products Carnivore Vitamin Spray
   For carnivorous and omnivorous reptiles
   Vitamins plus beta carotene

ESU Reptile Products Iguana Calcium
For iguanas and herbivorous reptiles
Calcium-phosphorus at a 2:1 balance
ESU Reptile Products Iguana Vitamin
For iguanas and herbivorous reptiles
Vitamins, minerals and amino acids
ESU Reptile Products Stress Ease
Reptiles and amphibians under stress
Vitamins and electrolytes
Four Paws Nature's Reptile Vita-Spray
For reptiles
Vitamins
Ocean Nutrition T-Rex Bio Series Bio-Vite
For all reptiles and amphibians
Broad-spectrum vitamin formula
Ocean Nutrition T-Rex Bio Series Bio-Vite Plus
For all reptiles and amphibians
Color-enhancing vitamin formula with beta carotene and vitamin C

Powders
Mardel Laboratories Formula C/P
For reptiles
Nutritional vitamin supplement with vitamin D
Mardel Laboratories Formula V/M/A
For lizards, snakes and turtles
Vitamins, minerals and amino acids
Nekton-Rep
For reptiles and amphibians
Vitamins, trace elements, amino acids and calcium
Nutri Grow Vitasaur
For reptiles
Multi-vitamin, mineral, amino acid, beta carotene and
   micronutrients
Ocean Nutrition T-Rex Calcium/Phosphorus 2:1
For herbivorous lizards, turtles, tortoises
Calcium/phosphorus supplement with vitamins
Ocean Nutrition T-Rex Calcium/No Phosphorus 2:0
For carnivorous lizards, turtles, snakes and amphibians
Calcium supplement, no phosphorus, plus vitamins

Rep-Cal
For reptiles
Phosphorus-free calcium supplement
Rep-Cal Herptivite
For reptiles
Vitamins, trace elements, beta carotene
Sticky Tongue Farms Secret Stash Miner-All
For reptiles and amphibians
Calcium and mineral supplement, phosphorus free
Tetra Reptovit
For all land reptiles
Calcium and phosphates, trace elements and vitamins
Zoo Med Reptivite
For reptiles
Vitamins, minerals, amino acids

CHART 13
MISCELLANEOUS REPTILE PRODUCTS

ESU Reptile Products Gut Load
Cricket and insect food
ESU Reptile Products Reptile Rinse
Spray that eliminates mites and ticks
ESU Reptile Products Shed Ease
Spray for ease in shedding old skin
ESU Reptile Products Terrarium Cleaner
Nontoxic cleaning and deodorizing spray for cleaning cages
ESU Reptile Products Tropical Mist
*Spray for tropical, high-humidity reptiles containing plant extracts
and aloe vera*
Ocean Nutrition T-Rex Bio Series Desert Formula
Odor-inhibiting/environment-refreshing spray for reptile cages
Ocean Nutrition T-Rex Bio Series Tropical Formula
Odor-inhibiting/environment-refreshing spray for reptile cages

TWELVE

FEEDING YOUR REPTILE

This may seem like the simplest and most obvious part of providing for your reptile's eating needs, but it, too, can be confusing. There are choices to be made about

- when to feed
- how to feed
- where to feed
- how much to feed
- how often to feed
- how to evaluate the food
- what to do when you wish to change foods

All these things contribute to your reptile's health.

HOW TO FEED?

With most reptiles, all you need to do is put the food in front of them. With reptiles that eat live mice or rats, or pre-killed mice or rats, use tweezers to grab the rodent's tail so that you can dangle the rodent in front of the reptile, letting go when the reptile grabs it.

If your reptile eats insects, you can offer them in a small, shallow bowl or plastic lid, such as a peanut butter jar lid. Or you can let the insects loose in the reptile's cage so that the reptile can hunt for them.

If you have herbivores, offer the food on a small paper plate or a shallow dish or on the floor of the cage. If you have outside tortoises, offer the food on a paper plate or on the grass.

WHEN TO FEED?

Most reptiles need warmth to stimulate their desire to eat. They also need warmth to digest the food that has been ingested. It's best to feed in the late morning, if possible, or midday. If you work during the day and it is not possible to feed during the heat of the day, put the food in your reptile's cage when you leave in the morning so that the animal can eat as it warms up during the day.

Some reptiles are stimulated to eat by other environmental factors. Argentine horned frogs, for example, will "wake up" and eat if sprayed lightly with warm water. Box turtles will eagerly eat after a rainfall or, if in captivity in the backyard, after the sprinklers have been on.

WHERE TO FEED?

Most reptiles will eat where they live, in their cage or enclosure. However, sometimes it's better to feed your reptile somewhere else. For example, some snakes are better off fed in another enclosure, other than their living enclosure. If you offer food by hand (or by tweezers), some snakes learn to anticipate food when your hand reaches into the cage and will begin striking at your hand. In those instances, it's much better to transfer the snake to another enclosure (or even a brown paper bag) and offer the food there.

HOW MUCH TO FEED?

This can be a difficult question to answer and is the question asked of most experienced reptile keepers and veterinarians. Obesity is a growing problem with reptiles and many have died of obesity-related health problems.

There is, unfortunately, no standard of measurement as to how much food any one reptile should eat. Factors include the reptile's species and type, activity level, environment (including temperature), age, state of health and more. For those reasons, the only guideline you really have is to feed enough food to keep your reptile happy and healthy, but not fat.

HOW OFTEN TO FEED?

Again, there is no one answer to this question. Most snakes will eat once a week. However, larger snakes eating larger meals may eat every other week and hatchling snakes might need to eat twice a week.

Larger frogs may eat once a week. Insectivores will usually eat daily, even several times a day, as will most herbivores.

CHANGING YOUR REPTILE'S FOOD

If you decide to change the food you are feeding your reptile, don't make the change abruptly. Many reptiles will refuse to eat when their food is changed and others will suffer severe gastrointestinal upset, complete with diarrhea and sometimes even vomiting. Changes in the reptile's diet must be made gradually.

If you are adding a commercially prepared food or are adding a new ingredient to a herbivore or omnivore's diet, make the change over a three-week period. Depending upon what your plans are for the new food or ingredient, add by small increments, gradually increasing the amounts over three weeks.

If you are changing an insectivore's diet, perhaps adding a different type of insect, start by introducing the new insect when the reptile is hungry. Make sure the reptile eats, though—it may or may not recognize the new insect as a food item and may go hungry. You may want to continue with the old food insects while introducing the new.

EVALUATING THE RESULTS

- Does your reptile look healthy? Does the skin look good or is it dull looking?
- Does the skin look smooth and filled out or is it bunchy, with unusual-looking folds?
- Are your reptile's eyes bright and alert?
- Is your reptile at a good weight, neither too fat nor too thin?
- Is your reptile eating all or most of its food?
- Is your reptile's activity level normal or better than it used to be? Is it normal for its species?
- Are your reptile's stools normal for its species? Has there been any change in the stools?
- Is the reptile being used in breeding program? If so, is it showing normal sex drive? Is it reproducing well? Are the offspring healthy?

If you can answer all these questions and your reptile appears healthy and of good weight and is reproducing well (if that is one of your goals), then you are probably feeding your reptile properly.

CHART 14
RECOMMENDED FOODS FOR AMPHIBIANS

Common Name *(Scientific name)*

Natural foods that can be fed in captivity. (Commercially prepared foods or supplements; note that vitamin-calcium supplements are recommended weekly unless stated otherwise.)

Frogs and Toads

Bullfrog: African *(Pyxicephalus adspersus)*

Crickets, earthworms, and other insects. When small can take pinkie mice; adults can eat larger mice. (May be fed T-Rex Snake Steak Sausage, a mouse-substitute food.)

Frog: Chilean Wide-Mouth *(Caudiverbera caudiverbera)*

Juveniles: a variety of insects, including earthworms, large crickets and small pinkie mice; fed daily. Adults: appropriate-size mice, young rats, goldfish; fed weekly (may be fed T-Rex Snake Steak Sausage, a mouse-substitute food.)

Frog: Leopard *(Rana pipens)*

A variety of appropriate-size insects.

Frog: Poison Arrow *(Dendrobatidae)*

A variety of small insects, including small crickets, mini-mealworms, fruit flies and ants.

Frog: Rubber *(Phrynomerus bifasciatus)*

A variety of small insects, including small crickets.

Frog: Tomato *(Dyscophus antongili)*

Juveniles: appropriate-size crickets and other insects; daily. Adults: larger crickets, other insects, small pinky mice; weekly.

Frog: Tropical Clawed *(Xenopus tropicalis)*

Aquatic foods, including tubiflex worms, brine shrimp, goldfish and guppies. (May take floating fish food, dried or freeze-dried fish and reptile foods as a supplemental feeding.)

Horned frog: Argentine *(Ceratophrys ornata)*
Froglets: goldfish, crickets, pinky mice; every two days. Juveniles: appropriate-size mice, goldfish; every three or four days. Adults: mice; weekly. (Some have been fed a commercial mouse-substitute food, such as T-Rex Snake Steak Sausage.)

Toad: European Common *(Bufo bufo)*
A variety of insects, including crickets, mealworms, waxworms and butterworms.

Toad: Fire-Bellied *(Bombina orientalis)*
Appropriate-size small insects, including small earthworms, tubiflex worms and brine shrimp. (May be offered floating fish-food flakes as a supplemental feeding.)

Toad: Midwife *(Alytes obstetricians)*
A variety of appropriate-size insects, including crickets, flies, mealworms and roaches.

Treefrog: Green *(Hyla cinerea)*
Appropriate-size crickets, mealworms, waxworms or other insects.

Treefrog: White's *(Litopia caerulea)*
Appropriate-size crickets, mealworms, king mealworms, waxworms and other insects. Large adults may be fed small pinky mice.

Newts and Salamanders
Newt: California *(Taricha torosa)*
A variety of appropriate-size insects, including earthworms, mealworms and crickets.

Newt: Chinese Emperor *(Tylototriton verrucosus)*
Crickets, earthworms, waxworms and other insects.

Newt: Eastern *(Notophalmus viridisceris)*
Small earthworms, small insects, tubiflex worms, blackworms, crickets and other small insects. (May be encouraged to eat fish-food flakes, dried or freeze-dried fish and reptile foods for supplemental feeding.)

CHART 14, CONTINUED

Newt: Marbled *(Triturus marmoratus)*
A variety of insects, including earthworms, mealworms and crickets.

Newt: Red-Spotted *(Notophthalmus viridescens)*
Aquatic foods, including tubiflex worms and brine shrimp as well as small insects, including appropriate-size mini-mealworms and earthworms.

Newt: Ribbed *(Pleurodeles waltl)*
Earthworms, snails, tubiflex worms, crickets and other insects.

Newt: Rough *(Pleurodeles waltl)*
Larger earthworms, nightcrawlers, mealworms, crickets and other insects. (May take fish-food flakes, dried or freeze-dried fish and reptile foods as a supplemental feeding.)

Newt: Smooth *(Triturus vulgaris)*
A variety of small insects, including small earthworms, mealworms, crickets and waxworms.

Salamander: Alpine *(Salamandra atra)*
Earthworms, crickets and other insects. (May eat fish-food flakes, dried or freeze-dried fish or reptile foods for supplemental feeding.)

Salamander: Dusky *(Desmognathus fuscus)*
A variety of insects, including earthworms, waxworms, mealworms and crickets.

Salamander: Fire *(Salamandra salamandra)*
Earthworms, crickets and other insects. (May take fish-food flakes, dried or freeze-dried fish and reptile foods for supplemental feeding.)

Salamander: Marbled *(Ambystoma opacum)*
A variety of small insects, including small earthworms, crickets and mini-mealworms.

Salamander: Mudpuppy *(Necturus maculosus)*
A variety of aquatic foods and insects as well as small fish. May be fed tubiflex worms, earthworms and small goldfish or guppies. (May be encouraged to eat fish-food flakes, dried or freeze-dried fish and reptile foods for supplemental feeding.)

Salamander: Siberian *(Hynobius keyserlingii)*
Earthworms, crickets, and other insects. (May take fish-food flakes, dried or freeze-dried fish and reptile foods as a supplemental feeding.)

Salamander: Spectacled *(Salamandrina terdigitata)*
Earthworms, crickets and other insects. (May take thawed-out frozen fish and reptile foods for variety.)

Salamander: Tiger *(Ambystoma tigrinum)*
A variety of larger insects, including larger earthworms, night-crawlers and crickets. (May be encouraged to eat floating fish foods or freeze-dried fish and reptile foods as a supplemental feeding.)

Axolotls
Axolotl: "Water Dog" or "Mudpuppy" *(Ambystoma mexicanum)*
Earthworms, goldfish, guppies. (May eat floating fish food or dried or freeze-dried fish and reptile foods as a supplemental feeding.)

CHART 15
RECOMMENDED FOODS FOR LIZARDS, GECKOS, CHAMELEONS AND RELATED PETS

Common Name *(Scientific name)*
Natural foods that can be fed in captivity. (Commercial foods or supplements; note that reptiles should be fed a vitamin-calcium supplement weekly unless otherwise noted.)

Anole: Green *(Anolis carolinensis)*
Small to medium-sized crickets, mini-mealworms, waxworms, butterworms.

CHART 15, CONTINUED

Alligator Lizard *(Gerrhonotus sp.)*
  Mice, chicks, insects, snails. (May be taught to accept mouse substitutes or chopped meat.)

Basilisk *(Basiliscus sp.)*
  Small mice, insects, vegetables, some fruit.

Bearded Dragon. *(Pogona vitticeps)*
  Crickets, waxworms, butterworms, pinkie mice; vegetation, including chopped mixed vegetables, grated squash, carrots; sweet fruits, such as melons. (All foods should be dusted weekly with a vitamin/calcium supplement designed for chameleons. Sometimes suffer from vitamin A toxicity. May eat a soaked, fruit-scented commercial food, such as T-Rex's Iguana food or Pretty Baby Iguana food or T-Rex's mouse substitute, Snake Steak Sausages.)

Chameleon: Jackson *(Chamaeleo jacksoni)*
  Appropriate-size crickets, mini-mealworms, waxworms, roaches, slugs and other insects. (Feed a supplement designed specifically for chameleons, such as Sticky Tongue Farms Miner-All. May suffer from vitamin A toxicity if oversupplemented.)

Chameleon: Panther *(Chamaeleo pardalis)*
  Appropriate-size crickets, flies, waxworms, mealworms and other insects.

Chameleon: Veiled *(Chamaeleo calyptratus)*
  Appropriate-size crickets, flies, mini-mealworms, waxworms, roaches and other insects.

Gecko: Day *(Phelsuma madagascariensis)*
  Small crickets, mini-mealworms, waxworms; sweet fruits, including baby food fruit. (May eat soaked fruit-scented prepared commercial foods, such as T-Rex Iguana Fruit and Flower formula or Zoo Med Iguana foods.)

Gecko: Flying *(Ptychozoon sp.)*
  Small crickets, mini-mealworms, waxworms and other small insects.

Gecko: Green Tree *(Naultinus elegans)*
    Small crickets, flies and other small insects; sweet fruits, including baby food fruits. (May eat a fruit-scented, commercially prepared food such as Pretty Baby Iguana food or T-Rex Iguana food.)

Gecko: House *(Hemidactylus garnoti)*
    Small insects.

Gecko: Leopard *(Eublepharis macularius)*
    Crickets and other appropriate-size insects.

Gecko: Tokay *(Gecko gecko)*
    Crickets, mealworms, kingworms, roaches, pinkie mice.

Iguana: Green *(Iguana iguana)*
    A variety of dark-green vegetables, grated squash, zucchini, carrots, yams. (May be fed one of the many commercially prepared foods specifically for iguanas; see Charts 7 and 8 in Chapter 8 and Chart 9 in Chapter 10.)

Lizard: Eastern Collared *(Crotaphytus collaris)*
    Crickets, mealworms, waxworms, butterworms; small pinkie mice.

Lizard: Long-Tailed Grass *(Takydromus sexlineatus)*
    Small crickets, mini-mealworms, waxworms, butterworms.

Lizard: Plated *(Zonosaurus ornatus)*
    Crickets, waxworms and other small insects; sweet fruit. May sometimes accept baby food fruit.

Lizard: Southern Alligator *(Elgaria multicarinata)*
    Crickets, mealworms, waxworms and other insects.

Lizard: Spiney *(Liolaemus sp.)*
    Small crickets, waxworms, and other small insects.

Lizard: Uromastix *(Uromastix acanthinurus)*
    Waxworms, butterworms, appropriate-size insects; vegetation, including red- and green-leaf lettuce, green and wax beans, yellow squash. May accept baby food vegetables.

CHART 15, CONTINUED

Monitor: Salvator *(Varanus salvator)*
Appropriate-size insects or rodents. (Lean meat, pre-killed frozen mice or rats, T-Rex frozen Snake Steak Sausages, Zoo Med canned monitor food, T-Rex Monitor Munch.)

Monitor: Savannah *(Varanus exanthematicus)*
Appropriate-size insects or rodents; snails, pinkie mice.
(Pre-killed frozen mice or rats, T-Rex frozen Snake Steak Sausages, Zoo Med canned monitor food, T-Rex Monitor Munch.)

Skink: Blue-Tongued *(Tiliqua scincoides)*
Crickets, snails, slugs, roaches and other insects; pinkie mice; vegetation, including chopped mixed vegetables and grated squash.

Skink: Fire *(Riopa fernandi)*
Small crickets, mini-mealworms, butterworms and other small insects.

Skink: Gold Grass *(Mabuya macularia)*
Small crickets and other insects.

Skink: Solomon Island Giant *(Corucia zebrata)*
Vegetation, including chopped mixed vegetables. (May eat a soaked, fruit-scented commercial food such as T-Rex Iguana food or Pretty Baby Iguana food.)

Swift: Jeweled *(Liolaemus tenius)*
Small crickets, waxworms and other small insects.

Tegu: Dwarf *(Callopistes maculatus)*
Appropriate-size insects, butterworms, raw eggs. (Canned tegu food, like Zoo Med.)

CHART 16
RECOMMENDED FOODS FOR SNAKES

Common Name *(Scientific name)*
Natural Foods that can be fed in captivity. (Commercially prepared foods or supplements; note that vitamin-calcium supplements are

recommended for snakes eating pinkie mice, fish or lizards; supplements are not normally recommended for snakes eating adult mice, rats, rabbits or other mammals.)

Anaconda *(Eunectes murinus)*
   Small to large mammals, eggs, fish.

Boa: Columbian *(Boa constrictor imperator)*
   Mice, rats, chicks. (May be fed T-Rex Snake Steak Sausage mouse-substitute food.)

Boa: Emerald *(Corallus caninus)*
   Mice, rats, chicks.

Boa: Rainbow *(Epicrates cenchria)*
   Mice, rats, chicks. (May be taught to eat mice-substitute foods.)

Boa: Red-Tailed *(Boa constrictor constrictor)*
   Mice, rats, small rabbits. (Hatchlings may be taught to eat mouse-substitute foods.)

Boa: Rosy *(Lichanura trivirgata)*
   Small mice. (May learn to accept mouse-substitute foods.)

Boa: Sand *(Eryx jaculus)*
   Pinkie and fuzzy mice. Often a very secretive eater. Will not eat if disturbed.

Bull Snake *(Pituophis melanoleucus)*
   Mice, rats, chicks.

Corn Snake *(Elaphe guttata)*
   Mice, lizards, frogs. (May be coaxed into eating mouse-substitute foods.)

Garter Snake *(Thamnophis)*
   Fish, amphibians, earthworms.

Gopher Snake *(Pituophis melanoleucus)*
   Mice, rats, chicks, lizards, other snakes.

CHART 16, CONTINUED

Grass Snake *(Natrix natrix)*
  Fish, amphibians, small mice.

Hognose Snake *(Heterodon)*
  Primary food is toads, although many will readily accept mice.
(Some have been switched to mouse-substitute foods with little
problem.)

Indigo Snake *(Drymarchon corais)*
  Mice, rats, fish, frogs, lizards.

Kingsnake: Common *(Lampropeltis getulus)*
  Mice, lizards and other snakes. (Unusually good eater in captivity.)

Milk Snake *(Lampropeltis triangulum)*
  Small to large mice, lizards. (Will often accept mouse-substitute
foods.)

Pine Snake *(Pituophis melanoleucus)*
  Mice, rats, chicks.

Python: African Rock *(Python sebae)*
  Mice, rats, chicks, small rabbits. (May refuse to eat in the winter.)

Python: Blood *(Python curtus brongersmai)*
  Small mice, small to large rats, small rabbits.

Python: Burmese *(Python molurus bivittatus)*
  Small juveniles: mice or small rats. Medium to large juveniles: rats.
Adults: rats, rabbits, chickens. (Juveniles may also be fed T-Rex Snake
Steak Sausage, mouse or rat size.)

Python: Burrowing *(Calbaria reinhardti)*
  Mice or lizards. (Can be a picky eater. Will rarely accept pre-killed
prey or mouse substitutes.)

Python: Reticulated *(Python reticulatus)*
  Juveniles: mice and rats. Adults: rats, rabbits, chickens.

Python: Royal or Ball *(Python regius)*
   Small to large mice, rats, chicks. (Known to be a difficult eater; will often fast for long periods of time. May be coaxed to eat mouse-substitute foods.)

Racer *(Coluber constrictor)*
   Lizards, frogs, mice. (Often a poor eater in captivity.)

Rat Snake *(Elaphe obsoleta)*
   Small to large mice, small rats. (May be coaxed to eat mouse-substitute foods.)

Rat Snake: Trans-Pecos *(Elaphe subocularis)*
   Pinkie mice for young snakes, small to large mice for adults.

Ribbon Snake *(Thamnophis sp.)*
   Mice, lizards, amphibians, fish.

CHART 17
RECOMMENDED FOODS FOR TORTOISES

Common Name *(Scientific name)*
   Natural foods that can be fed in captivity. (Commercially prepared foods or supplements; note that all foods should be dusted twice weekly with a vitamin-calcium supplement.)

Tortoise: Chaco *(Chelonoidis chilensis)*
   Insects, flowers, fruits, vegetation. (Prepared tortoise foods.)

Tortoise: Egyptian *(Testudo kleinmanni)*
   Fruit, flowers, vegetation, some insects. (Prepared tortoise foods.)

Tortoise: Elongated *(Geochelone elongata)*
   Vegetation, flowers, some fruit, some insects. (Prepared tortoise foods.)

Tortoise: Galapagos *(Geochelone elephantopus)*
   Vegetation, flowers, fruit, insects, some meat or carrion. (Prepared tortoise foods.)

CHART 17, CONTINUED

Tortoise: Gopher *(Gopherus polyphemus)*
   Vegetation, flowers, fruit, insects, some meat or carrion. (Prepared tortoise foods.)

Tortoise: Greek *(Testudo graeca)*
   Vegetation, flowers, some fruit, insects, some meat or carrion. (Prepared tortoise foods.)

Tortoise: Hermann's *(Testudo hermanni)*
   Grass for grazing, weeds, some flowers; chopped mixed dark-green vegetables, grated squash. (Prepared tortoise foods.)

Tortoise: Hingeback *(Kinezys sp.)*
   Vegetation, some flowers, fruits, some meat or carrion. (Prepared tortoise foods.)

Tortoise: Leopard *(Geochelone pardalis)*
   Grass for grazing, alfalfa, weeds, hibiscus flowers, rose blossoms; chopped mixed dark-green vegetables, grated squash, carrots; cactus pads; strawberries, bananas, tomatoes. (Prepared tortoise food.)

Tortoise: Marginated *(Testudo marginata)*
   Grass for grazing, weeds, hibiscus flowers; chopped mixed dark-green vegetables, grated squash. (Prepared tortoise food.)

Tortoise: Pancake *(Malocochersus tornieri)*
   Grass for grazing, weeds, seeds, succulents, alfalfa; mixed, chopped dark-green vegetables, grated squash. (Prepared tortoise food.)

Tortoise: Radiated *(Geochelone radiata)*
   Grass for grazing, weeds, some flowers; strawberries, bananas, some berries; chopped mixed dark-green vegetables, grated squash. (Prepared tortoise food.)

Tortoise: Russian *(Testudo horsfieldi)*
   Some meat or carrion; zucchini, squash, vegetables; hibiscus and rose blossoms; soaked dog food kibble. (Prepared tortoise food.)

Tortoise: Spurred *(Geochelone sulcatta)*
Grass for grazing, weeds, cactus, succulents; chopped mixed dark-green vegetables, grated squash, carrots; some fruits; *no citrus*. (Prepared tortoise food.)

Tortoise: Star *(Geochelone elegans)*
Grass for grazing, weeds, some flowers; chopped mixed dark-green vegetables; some fruits and berries. (Prepared tortoise food.)

Tortoise: Yellow-Foot *(Geochelone denticulata)*
Grass for grazing, weeds, clover; chopped mixed dark-green vegetables; grated squash, carrots; strawberries, bananas, tomatoes; some meat or carrion. (Prepared tortoise food.)

CHART 18
RECOMMENDED FOODS FOR TURTLES

Common Name *(Scientific name)*
Natural foods that can be fed in captivity. (Commercially prepared foods or supplements; note that turtles eating insects or fish should get a vitamin-calcium supplement twice weekly, but those eating commercial turtle foods or meat usually don't need it.)

Slider: Red-Eared *(Pseudemys scripta elegans)*
Insects, including earthworms, mealworms, crickets, snails and slugs; goldfish and guppies. (Will do well when switched over to a commercial turtle food.)

Turtle: Amboina Box *(Cuora amboinensis)*
Goldfish, guppies, insects; soft fruits, such as strawberries or plums, and vegetables. (Can also be fed a floating turtle food for water turtles or a commercial box turtle food.)

Turtle: Chinese Box *(Cuora flavomarginata)*
Insects, earthworms, snails, slugs, roaches and other insects; small pinkie mice; vegetables; fruits. (Can be fed commercial box turtle food, such as T-Rex Box Turtle food or Zoo Med Box Turtle food.)

CHART 18, CONTINUED

Turtle: Eastern Box *(Terrapene carolina carolina)*
  Insects, including crickets, mealworms, earthworms, snails, slugs and roaches; strawberries, tomatoes, yams, bananas and mixed chopped green vegetables. (May be fed a commercial box turtle formula.)

Turtle: Gulf Coast Box *(Terrapene carolina major)*
  Insects, including earthworms, crickets, mealworms, snails and slugs; strawberries, bananas and tomatoes. (May be fed a commercial box turtle food.)

Turtle: Mississippi Map *(Graptemys kohnii)*
  Insects, including crickets, earthworms and snails; goldfish or guppies. (Often do better in captivity when switched over to a commercial water turtle diet.)

Turtle: Ornate Box *(Terrapene ornata)*
  Insects, including crickets, mealworms, earthworms, snails and slugs; strawberries, tomatoes. (May be fed a commercial box turtle formula.)

Turtle: Painted *(Chrysemys picta)*
  Insects and small fish, but also some vegetables. (Will thrive on commercial turtle foods.)

Turtle: Reeve's *(Chinemys reevesi)*
  Insects, including earthworms and crickets; goldfish and feeder guppies. (May also be fed a floating fish or water turtle food.)

Turtle: Spiny Softshell *(Trionyx spiniferus)*
  Goldfish and feeder guppies. (Do better in captivity when switched over to a commercial water turtle food.)

Turtle: Spotted *(Clemmys guttata)*
  Insects, including earthworms, mealworms, crickets, snails and slugs; goldfish and guppies. (Will usually adapt easily to commercial turtle foods.)

Turtle: Three-Toed Box *(Terrapene carolina triunguis)*

Insects, including crickets, earthworms, mealworms, snails and slugs; strawberries, bananas and tomatoes. (Can be fed a commercial box turtle food.)

Turtle: Wood *(Clemmys insculpta)*

Insects, including earthworms, crickets, mealworms and roaches; goldfish and guppies; strawberries, bananas and other sweet fruits.

APPENDIX I

RECOMMENDED READING

One way to learn more about the specific needs of your reptile(s) is to read. There are three magazines on the market today that feature well-researched articles about reptiles, both the ones commonly kept as pets and the less commonly seen animals. I have also listed some books you would find helpful in caring for your reptile(s).

MAGAZINES

Reptiles
Fancy Publications
P.O. Box 58700
Boulder, CO 80322-8700

Reptile & Amphibian
RD 3, Box 3709-A
Pottsville, PA 17901

The Vivarium
American Federation of Herpetoculturists
P.O. Box 300067
Escondido, CA 92030-0067

BOOKS

Flank, Lenny, Jr. *The Snake: An Owner's Guide to a Happy Healthy Pet.* New York: Howell Book House, 1996.

——————. *The Turtle & Tortoise: An Owner's Guide to a Happy Healthy Pet.* New York: Howell Book House, 1997.

Rosenthal, Karen, DVM. *The Iguana: An Owner's Guide to a Happy Healthy Pet.* New York: Howell Book House, 1996.

Siino, Betsy Sikora. *You Want a What for a Pet?! A Guide to 12 Alternative Pets.* New York: Howell Book House, 1996. Includes information on iguanas, ball pythons, frogs and toads, turtles and tortoises, and salamanders.

APPENDIX II

MANUFACTURERS AND PROVIDERS OF REPTILE FOODS

MAKERS OR DISTRIBUTORS OF REPTILE FOODS AND SUPPLEMENTS

MANUFACTURER	PHONE NUMBER
Five Star Diets	800-747-0557
Kaytee	800-KAYTEE-1
LM Tropical Magic	800-332-5623
Nekton Rep USA	813-530-3500
Nutri Grow Premium Reptile Diets	800-737-8465
Ocean Nutrition T-Rex	800-275-7186
Pretty Pets	800-356-5020
Rep-Cal	408-356-4289
San Francisco Bay Brand	510-792-7200
Sticky Tongue Farms	909-672-3876
Zoo Med	805-542-9988

SOURCES OF LIVE FOODS FOR CARNIVORES

COMPANY	PHONE NUMBER	FOODS AVAILABLE*
G&A Frozen Rodents	718-456-0667	frozen mice, rats, chicks
The Gourmet Rodent	904-495-9024	mice, rats
Gretlo Kennel	310-328-2040	live mice, rats
The Iguana Farm	610-582-7825	frozen mice
MZ Enterprises	615-687-0757	quail eggs, chicks, chickens, rabbits
Mice Unlimited	800-642-3469	live and frozen mice
Mighty Mice	702-658-0921	live and frozen mice, rats
The Mouse Factory	915-837-7100	frozen mice, rats
The Mouse Trap	503-824-6423	frozen mice
Ocean Nutrition	619-336-4728	frozen mice, rats
Rodent Exchange	203-859-1704	frozen mice, rats, chicks
Sand Valley Farms	717-694-3759	mice, rats
Superior Rodents	415-452-3170	frozen mice, rats
Trans-Pecos Rat	915-837-2928	frozen rats

Note: Live feeder mice, rats and fish are often available at your local pet store.

SOURCES OF LIVE FOODS FOR INSECTIVORES

COMPANY	PHONE NUMBER	FOODS AVAILABLE*
Arbico	800-827-2847	crickets, waxworms, mealworms, flies
Bassett's	800-634-2445	crickets, mealworms
Drosophila	800-545-2303	fruitflies
Fluker Farms	800-735-8537	crickets, mealworms
Grubco	800-222-3563	mealworms, crickets, fly larva, waxworms, superworms
Holder	914-635-8471	cockroaches
Manchester Farms	800-497-8067	earthworms, red worms, nightcrawlers
Nature's Way	800-318-2611	mealworms, waxworms, fly larva, crickets
Rainbow Mealworms	310-635-1494	mealworms, crickets
Ray's Reptiles	402-477-1975	crickets, mealworms, waxworms
Rock Bottom Bait	904-463-7760	mealworms, waxworms, crickets
Testa	916-666-0321	houseflies, fruitflies
Top Hat Cricket	800-638-2555	crickets, mealworms, waxworms

*Note: Some pet stores may sell live insects.

BIBLIOGRAPHY

Alderton, David. *Turtles & Tortoises of the World.* New York: Facts on File Publications, 1988.

Ammer, Christine. *It's Raining Cats and Dogs.* New York: Dell Publishing, 1989.

Bartlett, Dick. "Small Tortoises in the Home Collection." *Reptiles,* April 1995, pp. 52–69.

Baumann, Mark. "Reptile Care Sheets." San Diego Herpetological Society, San Diego, Calif.

Bjorn, Byron. *Salamanders and Newts.* Neptune City, N.J.: TFH Publications, 1988.

Brown, Lauren E. "Successful Mealworm Raising." *Reptile & Amphibian,* March/April 1995, pp. 74–79.

Capula, Massimo. *Reptiles and Amphibians of the World.* John L. Behler, editor. New York: Simon & Schuster, 1989.

Comfort, David. *The First Pet History of the World.* New York: Simon & Schuster, A Fireside Book, 1994.

de Vosjoli, Phillipe. *The Box Turtle Manual.* Lakeside, Calif.: Advanced Vivarium Systems, The Herpetocultural Library Series, 1995.

————————. *The General Care and Maintenance of Box Turtles.* Lakeside, Calif.: Advanced Vivarium Systems, The Herpetocultural Library Series, 1991.

————————. *The Green Iguana Manual.* Lakeside, Calif.: Advanced Vivarium Systems, The Herpetocultural Library Series, 1992.

————————. *Horned Frogs.* Lakeside, Calif.: Advanced Vivarium Systems, The Herpetocultural Library Series, 1990.

————————. *Red-Tailed Boas.* Lakeside, Calif.: Advanced Vivarium Systems, The Herpetocultural Library Series, 1990.

Dolan, Edward F. *Animal Folklore.* New York: Ivy Books, 1992.

Dunne, Lavon J. *Nutrition Almanac,* 3rd ed. New York: McGraw-Hill Publishing, 1990.

Ford, Mark, DVM. "Reptile Medicine and Mineral Needs." In *Pet Lovers Handbook.* Cardiff, Calif.: Pet Lovers Publications, 1996.

Frye, Frederic L., DVM. *A Practical Guide for Feeding Captive Reptiles.* Malabar, Fla.: Krieger Publishing Co., 1993.

Hamdoun, Amro, and Dr. Frederic L. Frye. "Observations on the Growth of Juvenile Green Iguanas Fed Four Commercial Diets." *Vivarium* 7 (no. 2): 50–53.

Hewitt, Jef. *Keeping Unusual Animals as Pets.* New York: Sterling Publishing Co., 1991.

Highfield, A. C. *Keeping and Breeding Tortoises in Captivity.* London: R & A Publishing, 1990.

Hunziker, Ray. *Horned Frogs.* Neptune City, N.J.: TFH Publications, 1994.

"Lizard Care Sheet." Zoo Med, 3100 McMillan Rd., San Luis Obispo, CA 93401.

Mara, W. P. *Turtles as a Hobby*. Neptune City, N.J.: TFH Publications, 1993.

—————. *Turtles Yearbook*. Neptune City, N.J.: TFH Publications, 1993.

Masters, Charles O. *Encyclopedia of Live Foods*. Neptune City, N.J.: TFH Publications, 1975.

Mattison, Chris. *The Care of Reptiles and Amphibians in Captivity*. London: Blandford Press, 1990.

Nehring, Nancy. "Raising Fruit Flies." *Reptiles*, October 1995, pp. 26–30.

Obst, Fritz Jurgen. *Turtles, Tortoises and Terrapins*. New York: St Martin's Press, 1988.

Patterson, Jordan. *Box Turtles: Keeping and Breeding Them in Captivity*. Neptune City, N.J.: TFH Publications, 1994.

"Reptile Care Sheets." San Diego Herpetological Society, P.O. Box 4036, San Diego, CA 92164.

"Reptile Care Sheets." San Diego Turtle and Tortoise Society, 13963 Lyons Valley Rd., Jamul, CA 91935-9607.

Schmidt, W., K. Tamm, and W. Wallikewitz. *Chameleons*, vols. 1 and 2. Neptune City, N.J.: TFH Publications, 1994.

"Snake Care Sheet." Zoo Med, 3100 McMillan Rd., San Luis Obispo, CA 93401.

Walls, Jerry G. *Boas, Rosy and Ground*. Neptune City, N.J.: TFH Publications, 1994.

Wissman, Margaret, DVM, and Bill Parsons. "Metabolic Bone Disease in Green Iguanas." *Reptiles*, February 1994, pp. 68–72.

INDEX